KILL
THE DRUG TRADE

ENDING THE WAR ON DRUGS IN A SYSTEM OF
TOLERATION, COUNSELING AND CONTROL

Second Edition

DAVE FINCH

A System to Prevent Access by Minors, Reduce Addiction and
Crime, and End the Harms of Prison Terms for Drug Users

ISBN: 1976183111

ISBN 13: 9781976183119

Library of Congress Control Number: 2013917151
CreateSpace Independent Publishing Platform
North Charleston, South Carolina

Dedicated

*To my wife, Nancy and to our
boys, Michael, Jonathan and Matthew*

Acknowledgements

Though not in all cases in favor of my idea, the following generous experts have given me valuable information and suggestions. Each and all have contributed to my understanding and the quality of the book more than they know, and I am grateful to and thank them.

My editor, Susan Gabriel, Sierra Writers (President)
Dr. Jeffrey Kane, M.D.
Judge Candace Heidelberger
Judge Thomas Anderson
Judge Al Dover (Ret'd)
Judge James P. Gray (Ret'd)
Psychologist and author Tracy Deliman,
Mike Lambert. Wildwood Literary Review
And the many other fine authors and thinkers whose work has so well informed mine.

Table of Contents

Preface

The absurdity of national, indeed global, drug policy is too glaring to ignore. Drug abuse and addiction create blight in society, but use-prohibition has shown itself no help in eradicating it. The legalization/decriminalization vs. prohibition debate has become so polarized it crowds out consideration of combining modern skills and technologies in ways that present a workable alternative.

Among the many well-informed voices decrying our failed war on drugs is that of the 2011 Report of the Global Commission on Drug Use, among whose recommendations is the following:

> End the criminalization, marginalization and stigmatization of people who use drugs but who do no harm to others. Challenge rather than reinforce common misconceptions about drug markets, drug use and drug dependence.

This recommendation which gives support to the reform movement is excellent as far as it goes, but it goes little further than saying, for God's sake do something. This book offers a way to do something

There are many good books on drug policy, and I have learned a great deal from them and the scholarly literature on drug use and addiction. Some writers have come to within the near distance of the encompassing reform I propose. Yet none has suggested a system offering a comprehensive solution like that described here. My proposal is based upon the economic principle of market-force creative destruction – in this case black market destruction – in a system that features dispensation of legally and safely manufactured pharmaceuticals to those whose drug purchases otherwise support the drug trade: the tiny minority who make up the frequent and regular adult users and addicts.

Accompanied by practical control mechanisms, the system curtails dramatically the access young people now have to drugs. The vast numbers of teenage experimenters are the feedstock of the hard-core user and addict market. Take away teenage access to drugs and you will stem the flow of new customers into that market. Allow those already in the market to purchase legally manufactured drugs until they are ready for sobriety and you kill the illegal drug trade. Insist upon regular contact with trained counselors who are trained not to treat addiction, but to encourage and facilitate the seeking of recovery and you vastly improve the rate at which addiction is discovered and cured.

A second principle on which the proposal is based is that, because the laws against drugs so raise their street prices, the only way many addicts can afford them is to steal, deal or prostitute themselves. Providing these people with legal and affordable access to drugs will eliminate those perverse incentives and reduce crime.

A third principle is that a person whose dignity and self-esteem are intact is a contender for the prize of a healthy life, but one who is stigmatized and demoralized for drug use may struggle much longer to attain it. A person who is taken from the world of work and put in prison not only becomes poorer for it, but may remain long, or even permanently, unemployed thereafter. The poverty of a drug user is not conducive to seeking treatment, but a brighter future clearly is. Treating addiction as the health issue it is and allowing addicts to avoid stigma and to be productive members of society will promote recovery far more effectively than criminal punishment.

Finally, the System incorporates regular and frequent counseling because it is demonstrable that a great deal of continued addiction is the product of user ignorance about the nature of addiction and the pathways to recovery: an ignorance, alas, fostered by the media and even by professionals in the treatment industry who would like to see more addicts come their way. Counselors who provide a friendly and informative presence in the lives of addicts can provide, not treatment, but a great deal of friendly assistance in ways that encourage addiction recovery as we'll discuss in Chapters 7 and 8.

This book is not written from a viewpoint that considers drug use to be immoral. Try articulating a firm basis for branding immoral the mere use of drugs and you will not find it easy. The use of psychoactive drugs is a practice of ancient origin and is widespread in many cultures today. Drugs for many represent an effective and desirable means of coping with the challenges of human life, which others can address without them. Moreover, modern science has confirmed that some of the currently illegal drugs are beneficial to health and well-being. It is not the use of drugs that should be condemned, but their irresponsible use resulting in societal harm that we should try to curtail. In this purpose drug prohibition has failed, and for reasons discussed in this book, cannot do otherwise.

I have approached this work in some humility for I enter here a field in which so much scholarly and professional work has already been done. My qualifications for doing so include a multi- year interest in the topic; personal observations of friends, clients and others known to use drugs; interviews with judges, and other professionals; my legal credentials and study of economics, though I am in no sense to be considered an economist; incidental studies of human nature, and behavioral psychology; (human nature and psychology were always germane in the practice of law and my later practice of dispute mediation) and a broad reading of the literature in the field of drug policy. This resume is offered not to support a claim of expertise, but only that I have acquired the skills needed to present here material that is sometimes abstract and sometimes controversial.

There are strong, though refutable, arguments against even moderate, constrained and responsible use of psychotropic drugs for non-medicinal pleasure. These preconceptions lead to political obstacles. The dual purpose of this book is to shed more light on these, and to illustrate a pathway toward adequate balance between effective drug control, and our prized tradition of freedom of each to pursue his or her individual preferences.

The system proposed is a principled and humane alternative that will bring drug users, abusers and addicts into a confidential program that tolerates responsible use with counseling, a system I show to be economically and scientifically sound. Given the state of U.S. politics today one can only hope it is politically feasible, but the control mechanisms prescribed will foster wider acceptance than either legalization or decriminalization. This book is for readers at all levels of understanding as well as for officials, policy makers and politicians on whom we will have to rely to explain the idea and its rationale to their constituents. I hope that the reader will help spread the word that this System is needed and workable and consummately moral.

December 10, 2013

Dave Finch

PREFACE TO SECOND EDITION

The world turns and learns at a rapid pace. Since publication of the first edition of this book, the world has learned more. I have made numerous changes here a) to clarify some passages and b) to update the material. I have also changed the title of Chapter 1 from the overly optimistic "idea whose time is now" to a more grounded: A dynamic idea with power and impact. America seems unready for this idea in the "now," but as the pace of enlightenment quickens perhaps we can hope for change in the "soon."

July 23, 2017

Dave Finch

Chapter 1:

A dynamic idea with power and impact

If at first, the idea is not absurd, then there is no hope for it.

Albert Einstein

It takes considerable knowledge just to realize the extent of your own ignorance.

Thomas Sowell

Over the past half century, the barely audible voices of protest at the beginning of the war on drugs have grown to a high-volume chorus of opposition impossible to ignore. Some of the best minds in the world, representative of all points along the political spectrum, are voicing agreement with the conclusion of the 2011 Report of the Global Commission on Drug Policy[1] that the so-called war on drugs has not only failed, but continues to inflict devastating consequences on the lives of individuals and the health and safety of our communities. This report was joined in 2016 by the Lancet Commissions with their report titled "Public health and international drug policy."[2] Whereas the earlier report is the work of world leaders consisting of both conservatives and progressives, the Lancet report is the work of leading international scientists. Both reach the same conclusion–drug prohibition has got to go.

Most of us know something about the havoc delivered courtesy of the pursuit of drug prohibition. We'll detail it in chapters that follow. Allow me here to briefly identify the more prominent harms. They include: the corruption of officials all the way from the upper levels of government right down through the ranks to the cops on the street: corruption which has ensnared judges, prosecutors, prison guards, mayors, legislators and more; an incentive for addicted adults and youngsters alike to steal, burglarize, cheat, prostitute themselves and deal drugs for money to buy drugs; overcrowding of prisons and the inhumane warehousing of non-violent drug addicts; the ruining of employment chances by prosecution of people with productive potential; the fostering of business for cartels and large gangs so profitable they are able to buy guns, planes, "soldiers" and allies more than sufficient to overwhelm law enforcement; the engendering of wars between competing cartels, gangs and dealers resulting in the annual murder of tens of thousands of innocent people as well as the lawless; and the propagation of millions of small-scale dealers and user/dealers who provide easy drug access to minors.

It is this last point that makes the pursuit of prohibition wrong. As we cannot stop illegal traffickers from getting drugs into the hands of minors, nearly 200,000 new substance use disorders arise among them each year.

The lessons of history, which we learned with alcohol prohibition last century, led us to abandon that mistake in the early 1930s. It took us only eleven years of that folly to realize a law so out of "sync" with human nature causes more damage to individuals and communities than any measurable benefit. But, in fear they would destroy our culture, we continued the identical mistake in the laws against drugs. While many of us grasp the horrendous penalties we are paying for this mistake, too many do not and so the political paralysis continues.

Politicians win votes with emotional appeals for policies they think might help in the fight against addiction. Emotions have been inflamed by the news media and the myths of imagined "dope fiends" and "fried egg" brains and other stories that spice up media content. In our moral confusion and lack of scientific knowledge of the realities of drug use and addiction, we fail to demand of our leaders the kind of public debate and creative re-thinking needed to reverse the destructive course we still follow. Apparently, it seems to most people, even some who are experts in the field, that drug use prohibition is the only game in town.

This game costs us something in the neighborhood of $100 billion per year counting all costs at the local, state and federal government levels.[3] This means that over the next ten years taxpayers will spend a trillion dollars, just as we already have in the past 10. Over those past 10 years the drug use rates have remained essentially the same, but with the average age of initiation dropping to the 8th grade level.

It seems that our fear of what drugs do in society is so great it blinds us to the reality that prohibiting adult use fosters use also by minors and so creates more drug use. It does this by creating an underground illegal market, which minors can access— right along with the adults. As mentioned, this means that nearly 200,000 minors develop substance use disorders (SUDs) each year, graduating to adulthood to become profitable customers of drug peddlers. Teenagers are now using at the rate of 9.4% of the 12 through 17 age group. Between 10% and 20% of those adolescent users become addicted just as they are progressing to adulthood.[4]

According to SAMHSA, at the time of this writing, there are about 7.1 million in our country with substance use disorders involving the illegal drugs. or about 2% of our population. Despite the righteous stance of our government and politicians, millions of minors are accessing illegal drugs each year, with devastating consequences for some. Our fervid pursuit of adult use prohibition not only fails to protect adolescents, it fosters the very underworld industry that furnishes their means of self-destruction.

Surely, we must seek out a better way forward for controlling drugs than with the blunt tools of the criminal justice system. The health based System proposed in this book offers that better way.

Try suspending skepticism for a moment and follow me into an imaginary world in which young people under the age of 21 cannot get their hands on any drugs unless they beg, borrow or steal from adults and that has become very difficult because adult users are carefully guarding their limited legal supply; the number of adult drug users has dropped below current rates; most users do so responsibly, meaning they are maintaining stable and generally productive lives; users access a reliable supply of safely manufactured affordable drugs of certified potency and purity; addicts no longer steal, cheat or sell their sex to get money for drugs; the police now have more time to focus their attention upon illegal drug suppliers and all the other crimes; jails and prisons are no longer over-crowded; addicted parents instead of doing jail time are working and supporting their children; health care costs in the country have dropped due to higher rates of addiction recovery; state government budgets are free of the burden of enormous law enforcement and prison costs; the murder rates in the U.S. and Mexico have fallen to lows not seen for decades; police corruption has plummeted; the kingpins of the drug cartels and gangs have stopped trying to make money on drugs in the U.S.

Impossible you say? In the pages that follow you will find this picture, or something very much like it, to be an expectable result of the dynamic System I propose. We can create that world if we will heed the lessons of history; toss out biased and myth-based beliefs about drugs; and recombine the talents and technologies at our disposal in the modern world.

The dynamic idea

The fundamental premise of the idea may be the hardest for many to believe: we cannot keep drugs out of the hands of minors unless we tolerate drug use by adults. This book shows its truth. The second premise is that the protection of minors against addiction is paramount under any drug policy. Nine in ten addicts got that way by starting drug use between the ages of 12 and 17.[5] One in four Americans who began using any addictive substance before age 18 are addicted, compared to 1 in 25, who started at age 21 or older.[6] The question before the country, is how do we allow adults to use drugs, without them leaking into the hands of minors.

The answer this book offers – pared to its essential elements– is this:

Adult drug users become clients of a drug dispensary service operated by an entity which delivers legally manufactured drugs of certified potency and purity, at regular intervals, and at below street prices to most and free to some. Clients commit to responsible use, the following of certain rules, random blood or urine testing (to discourage excessive use) and regular ongoing contact with counselors who keep them informed of relevant drug knowledge, and treatment options. Clients who play by the rules no longer fear prosecution, but those who fail to abide by the program's rules are subject to ouster from it. Preventing access to drugs by minors is emphasized.

Any new and seemingly ambitious or radical idea will often be rejected out of hand by those who misinterpret it or the realities on which it is based. In Chapter 6, biases and irrationalities, which. to an extent, help maintain the status quo are discussed, as is the dynamism that underlies the change proposed. There are many reservations various people will have about this idea, all of which will be addressed along the way. These reservations include 1) a tolerant system will be enabling to addiction; 2) it will send the wrong signal to young people; 3) drug using parents will share with their kids and/or neglect them while using; 4) it will be too expensive to operate; 5) it will never be politically feasible; 6) it will add to the costs of health care; 7) it will produce more crime and violence; 8) and turn the country into a drug culture. These are legitimate concerns, but I show how the new System would aptly deal with each and all of them.

Throughout the book I use the capitalized word System to denote what I also sometimes refer to as the "proposed system" or the "System I propose."

Fact checking popular assumptions.

The public discourse on drug policy is based on various incorrect assumptions. Let's set the record straight on a few important ones.

1. **Drug users include, equally, all economic and racial groups.**

    As a thought experiment, picture in your mind the typical drug user. Then answer whether this person is employed full time, part time, or unemployed. Then choose which annual income level is closest to this person's: $20,000 or more than $50,000. Got the picture? I'll give a score of ten for the correct image. You get 5 points for seeing a white instead of a minority person, 2 ½ pts. for selecting employed full time. And if you picked more than $50,000 as closer than $20,000 to this person's income you get 2 ½ points. If you scored low, you are like me, before I did the research for this book.

    Drug use is not a behavior mostly of the poor and the minorities. More whites than blacks use illegal drugs and the per capita rate of use of the two groups is about equal. While poverty and privation certainly do play a role in drug use, as one might expect of a life oppressed by despair and boredom, on PBS Frontline in the winter of 1997-98, drug policy expert, Mark Kleiman said: "most people who are illicit drug users are employed, stable respectable citizens." Unfortunately, newscasts feature drug arrest stories more often occurring in minority neighborhoods, and in relation to crimes of various sorts. It should not surprise us that drugs are associated in the minds of most of us with poverty and crime.

2. The cause of addiction is not what you think

I'll bet more than 99% of Americans believe that using mind-altering drugs causes addiction. I believed that until I was well in to my studies of addiction. Science now shows something quite different. Most drug users do not become addicted. Some percentage, ranging from 10% to about 25%, depending how widely or narrowly addiction is defined, do fall into that trap.

So, what is it that causes addiction? The drug use is obviously part of it, but the critical part is vulnerability—a mental condition rendering an individual susceptible. Such vulnerabilities arise sometimes from personality development, which may stem from troubled childhood conditions, poor parenting, child abuse or other trauma. Genes sometimes play a role in this too. Some treating specialists such as Gabor Maté suggest drug dependence can always be traced back to childhood trauma.[7] But, NIDA Director Volkow and her colleagues tell us genetic variations can may also play a role.[8]

In a 2016 paper, Director Volkow and colleagues[9] explain that without vulnerability, drug use does not result in addiction, and that addiction occurs in only about 10% of users. They define addiction as the severe form of substance use disorder, discussed below.[10] In a textbook authored by Carl Hart and Charles Ksir, they speak of dependence (addiction) as an overwhelming involvement with getting and using drugs, as in recurrent over-eating or gambling.[11] But, all experts agree that mere drug use alone, absent vulnerability that promotes recurrent use despite harmful consequences does not cause addiction or dependence.

Addiction is a habit-like behavior in response to an urge so strong the person's self-control has been compromised. Evidence of this loss of control is present when the person uses despite wanting to quit, repeatedly uses more than intended or gives up other important activities in deference to the substance.[12] However, there are people who have become drug dependent, who do not exhibit those signs: they simply continue a habit they believe is critical in their lives. But, if they tried to quit they would not find it easy. For them the benefit outweighs the negative consequences.

The national survey SAMHSA, (Behavioral Health Trends in the United States: Results from the 2014 National Survey on Drug Use and Health) shows as of this writing, we have about 27 million current illegal drug users, age 12 and above, and about 7.1 million of those have a substance use disorder (SUD). Not all SUDs are necessarily addictions. SUDs are defined by the American Psychiatric Association in their DSM V publication, as a condition in which three of eleven diagnostic criteria are present.[13] I summarize those below. According to APA one must have 6 or more of those criteria present to qualify as a severe SUD. And Volkow, et. al. tell us they use the word addiction to refer only to those severe cases. We do not know how many SUDs are severe and therefore deemed to be addiction. But, even if we pretended all to be, we would have to say that only about 25% of current drug users are drug dependent or addicted.

In their paper, Volkow and colleagues say true addiction involves a substantial loss of self-control as indicated by compulsive drug taking despite the desire to quit. That is one of the APA's DSM V criteria for SUD. Two other criteria common in addiction are tolerance (needing more to get the same effect, and withdrawal (feeling sick when the drug is not used). This fits with what I sense is the most usual view of addiction. Some addictions do not involve the severe withdrawal symptoms common to the opioids and heroin. Meth and cocaine addicts experience tolerance, but do not fear sickness from withdrawal.

The other eight SUD criteria set out in DSM V can be summarized as: using more or for longer than intended; spending a lot of time getting, using, or recovering from drug use; cravings and urges to use; failing to manage obligations of work, home or school, because of use; continuing to use, even when it harms relationships; giving up important social, occupational or recreational activities because of drug use; using again and again, even when it poses danger; continuing to use despite a physical or psychological problem caused or worsened by the use.

The APA considers 2 or 3 of these symptoms to be a mild substance use disorder, 4 or 5 to be moderate, and 5 or more to be severe.

Before we leave this section, there is an additional insight that helps further illuminate the nature of addiction. Scientists speak of the role of dopamine in the brain. It's a natural chemical that stimulates activity in brain regions involved with habit and self-control. Stress triggers a dopamine reaction, which activates a region in the brain involved with coping habits. And so, if one feels stress, dopamine works to get her going on what is needed to relieve the stress. She is "coping" in her usual, habit based way. Drugs can induce dopamine release also and this can light up pleasure centers. In the initial stages of drug use the person feels a dopamine induced pleasure, but after a time, as Volkow, et. al., explain, it no longer works that way. Where a habit of using the drug has been formed, what has happened is the learning centers of the brain have become conditioned to coping with stress by using a drug—the coping method has become: "get the drug into my system." So even when the drug no longer produces pleasure, the addicted person *wants* it, just to relieve the stress.[14]Drug craving may often just be a matter of needing to cope with a stressful situation.

It is clear now that an addict's drug taking is not necessarily a case of seeking a high; it is more likely the medication of a stressful situation. This occurs with stimulants such as cocaine or methamphetamine, or narcotics like marijuana and heroin. Heroin and the opioids, however, do bring an additional dimension. If you don't take the drug after a period of regular use you get sick. Withdrawal from heroin and the opioids that imitate it can be quite distressing and the addicted put it off compulsively.

Why is all this important? The common assumption that drug taking is *the cause* of addiction discourages willingness to consider toleration of responsible adult drug use as a matter of policy. At the same time, we unfairly stigmatize repeat drug "offenders" by failing to understand addiction as a temporary mental disorder which is characterized by loss of self-control. The genetic factors and special vulnerabilities at the root of addiction explain both the intensity of drug craving and severity of withdrawal.[15] Shouldn't we conclude that making moral judgments against such troubled people is itself morally deficient?

3. **Using drugs for many is a rational decision and they do it responsibly**.

Rational drug use, as we discuss in Chapter 5, is use that confers a benefit which is not outweighed by negative consequences. Many use drugs without ruining social relationships, or materially weakening their ability to function normally and productively. Compare moderate alcohol use. Most of us accept that a drink or two for relaxation at the end of a day can be beneficial. The medical profession does not oppose moderate use of alcohol and total abstention is now even deemed a risk factor for various illnesses.

It is plausible to say that many adults who use drugs derive valuable relief of anxieties and stress. Not all drug taking is a bad idea. Among other things, the System proposed makes it possible to focus on those who are not using rationally, a fraction of the total user population. It is also plausible to say that some people, deprived of their preferred drug, turn to the generally more harmful (less rational) use of alcohol.

4. The association of drugs with crime is no reason to reject a use tolerant system.

A popular assumption is that drug users do terrible things and we tend to associate drug use with underworld activities. Yet, confusion surrounds the question of what induces a drug user to commit crime. Is it the pharmacological effect of the drug, or is something else at work?

Crime related to drug use falls into three categories. First there are crimes committed by addicts who cannot otherwise afford their drugs. Facing withdrawal or otherwise feeling a need of the drug, they commit crimes to buy drugs. These include the acquisitive crimes such as burglary, theft, armed robberies, car jackings, but also prostitution and small-scale drug dealing. The second category involves the crimes incident to the illegal drug trade itself, often violent, as dealers enforce their "rights" against each other and sometimes against their customers. Included here also are smuggling, bribing of officials, money laundering and the like.

Those first two categories account for all but a small percentage of criminal activity. The third category are the crimes thought to have been either induced or encouraged by the chemical effects of a drug—pharmacological effect. There is no clear evidence that drugs chemically induce otherwise honest people to behave criminally and as Hart and Ksir put it, "…it is incorrect to conclude that using any particular drug will turn a person into a criminal."[16] These experts point out that longitudinal studies of children and adolescents show tendencies toward crime and other anti-social behavior appear *before* first drug use.

Still drug use and personality disorders sometimes go together and it seems plausible that a drug such as a stimulant might embolden some to go over the line. For example, PCP can cause such a disorientation an arrestee may resist violently. While most crime in which drugs were involved can be explained on grounds other than the chemical effects of the drug, we cannot rule out the possibility that chemical effects play a causative role in some cases.

Does such a possibility suggest we should pause before moving to a drug tolerant program? Quite the opposite. Because anti-social tendencies can now be identified at early ages and increasingly records are available to identify those who have them, the System's monitoring feature would help to head off tendencies toward drug induced crime. The monitoring feature is discussed in Chapters 8 and 10. Moreover, by allowing drugs such as marijuana, cocaine, certain amphetamines and heroin, we would be allowing these users far better alternatives to the more dangerous types such as PCP.

So, here we see that we will have a more effective means to prevent chemically induced crime in a system that all but eliminates the major inducements to crime, namely, crime committed to buy drugs and crime related to dealing in drugs.

5.   Tolerating adult drug use will not produce more of it.

Most adults show no interest in the pleasures of drug taking at the risk of the negative consequences to normal life activities they bring. In Chapter 3 we discuss the countries whose liberalizing of drug use has not resulted in higher use rates. While a RAND study concluded that legalization of marijuana in California would result in increased use, statistical data in Holland, where all forms of cannabis are legal, show that among young people of the medium age 28 in the Netherlands, where cannabis products are sold in widely available "coffee shops." only 16% ever smoked marijuana.[17] Soft drugs when widely accessible seem to lose much of their appeal and there is no empirical evidence that toleration of their use results in increase. In fact, as we shall later see, under the proposed system there is reason to expect, over time, a reduction in adult use as users become better informed about how to use responsibly and far fewer minors have access to drugs on which to start use.

6. Addiction is treatable and can be resolved, usually by one's early thirties.

Despite the frequent claim that addiction is a lifetime disorder, most of the addicted recover without any recurring symptoms by their early thirties and many before that. Roughly 75% of people who are drug dependent by age 24 become symptom free by the age of 37.[18] It is important that addicts are given this information. Addicts who want to recover should not be discouraged from doing so by the belief in the old "once addicted, always addicted" assumption. There is ample reason for optimism that they will achieve complete recovery.

7. Addicts can live productive lives.

Some addicts will choose to continue to live with addiction in a use tolerant system, and do so as useful, productive members of society. Consider the case of one of the founders of the Johns Hopkins Hospital, the famed surgeon, Dr. William Halstead– praised by his peers for his technique and teaching. He first became addicted to cocaine while studying its anesthetic properties. Some close friends aggressively intervened and he stopped using cocaine, but unknown to most of them he began self-treating with morphine, an opiate. He carried on his surgical practice for decades as a morphine addict.[19] Other productive drug addicts include authors Stephen King and William Burroughs, Hunter Thompson; actors Alex Baldwin and Liz Taylor, famous funny man Robin Williams and a vast array of others who pursued their careers while dependent on drugs. Criminologists have found that addicts devote very little time to getting high and spend most of it working or hustling.[20] Wouldn't we prefer that they be allowed the chance to work productively, instead of hustling for drugs or the money to buy them? Drug use toleration accompanied by a robust counselling program is surely a better way to foster both responsible use and earlier quitting of drugs, than our criminal justice regime that forces them to get their drugs in the underworld.

The federal drug scheduling scheme

The Controlled Substances Act of 1970 in Title 21, Section 812, categorizes the many drugs into five schedules. The criteria for inclusion in each schedule are summarized as follows:

Schedule I drugs are those with no currently accepted medical use and a high potential for abuse. Placed in this category by the FDA were many opiates and opium derivatives and hallucinogens. Here you will find heroin, Ecstasy (MDMA), mescaline and peyote along with LSD and "marihuana". It seems absurd today that marijuana is listed here. The weight of authority is on the side of medically beneficial use of cannabis.

Schedule II includes drugs which in addition to having a high potential for abuse could potentially lead to severe psychological or physical dependence—also called addiction. Here we find cocaine and methamphetamine among others, including methadone which is used in the treatment of addiction.

The criteria for Schedule III drugs are that they have a potential for abuse, but one which is less than that for the first two schedules; that they have a currently accepted medical use; but "abuse" may lead to some low level of physical dependence or an elevated level of psychological dependence.

Schedule IV drugs are those that have accepted medical uses, but have a low potential for abuse and, compared to the drugs of the first three schedules, they lead to "limited" physical or psychological dependence.

Schedule V drugs are defined with criteria like those of Schedule IV, only they are less risky still.

It is to these schedules and the drugs placed by the government within them that various federal and state laws apply to ban their possession, and by extension, their use.

Each of the schedules speaks of potential for abuse, but it does not tell us how to quantify "high potential" or some other level of "potential" and it doesn't define abuse. Law professor Douglas Husak looked at the legislative history and found that Congress considered the potential for abuse to exist when some individuals were found to be taking a drug in sufficient quantities to risk harm to themselves or others; or when there is evidence of diversion of drugs from legitimate channels; or where individuals are initiating the drug use on their own without medical advice.[21]

Use, abuse and responsible use

That latter point, using without medical advice reflects a common understanding of drug abuse. You read articles in the paper and hear politicians speak of people "abusing" drugs. What they are saying is merely that they are using drugs illegally. In this book. I speak of drug use and substance use disorders. I seldom use drug abuse, which to me can only mean a disordered or irresponsible use. This is consistent with the position of the American Psychiatric Association (APA). They have abandoned the term altogether.

The term abuse appeared in the APA's diagnostic manual, DSM-IV up until 2013, under the heading Substance Abuse and Substance Dependence. It was defined as one or more of four criteria: use resulting in failure in obligations at work, school or home; use in situations where physically hazardous; recurrent use-related legal problems, or continued interpersonal (social) problems caused or worsened by the substance use.

But, the term "abuse" has been dropped from the medical vocabulary. In the APA's 2013 publication of DSM V, the single term "substance use disorder," was adopted. As mentioned above, it is defined as having three or more of eleven signs or symptoms.

Using drugs can be done in a rational, responsible way as we later discuss. Use that is not responsible includes consumption of drugs in such doses or frequency that the user's judgment is impaired and he or she engages in risky or socially offensive behaviors. It also includes driving while impaired, using in hazardous situations, neglecting children in the user's care, the persistent alienation of family, friends, and co-workers, and using drugs when they reduce the ability to perform one's job. This is what I would call drug abuse. Merely using should not be confused with abusing.

Can addicted persons use responsibly? In most cases, the answer is an emphatic yes. Most users and many addicts use responsibly, and those who don't can learn to do so. The common image of the doped-up loser staggering or slouching on the street characterizes some, but the majority are not like that. It is the addicts who use and behave irresponsibly in the way or under the circumstances in which they use, we should focus on. Teaching these people how and why to use responsibly is one of the key features of the proposed system, which also insists upon it.

Pursuing prohibition, we lose the benefit of federalism

Our pursuit of drug prohibition deprives us of the benefits of state experimentation with alternative policies. In drafting the Constitution, the founders were intent upon preserving federal and state separation. The 10th Amendment addressed it: powers not delegated to the U.S. government were reserved to the states and to the people. The idea was to keep government as close to the people as practicable. The famous social observer Alexis d'Tocqueville pointed out in the early 19th century that the several states serve as experimental laboratories for policies that might then be adopted beneficially in other states or even nationally.

Today those benefits of federalism are only awkwardly enjoyed in the case of drug policy. While several states have legalized recreational marijuana and more than half have legalized medical marijuana, they have done so despite the power of federal authorities to arrest and imprison people for possessing and selling it. In recent years, the U.S. Attorney General adopted a policy of benign neglect in those states, choosing to look the other way–but not in the others. There is an incoherence here, since marijuana is classified as a Schedule I drug–one lacking in any accepted medical use, and the Attorney General and the DEA have continued to maintain their power and right to investigate and raid those who possess it for sale. Even possession for medical purposes is a federal crime. As time passes the picture will surely clarify, but it strikes many of us as unfortunate the federal government so dominates the terrain of drug policy. The states could be trying new approaches to dealing with all the drugs and we could be learning how to control them without jailing people.

Chapter 2:

The Devastation We Live With

[Said of current political science, and applied here in the drug context, that it fiddles while Rome burns] "excused by two facts: it does not know that it fiddles, and it does not know that Rome burns.

Leo Strauss

Americans always do the right thing right after they have exhausted all the other options.

Winston Churchill

Resistance to change in our national drug policy comes from many quarters and various biases, but it seems likely that the inertia in America is to a considerable extent based on thinking something like this: *Even though there is a lot of unwanted drug use, our prohibition system seems to be keeping a lid on it, so why should we go to the bother of adopting radical change?* Anyone who thinks that way should pay attention to the international reports previously mentioned. For example, the 2011 Report of the Global Commission on Drug Use list of "devastating consequences" of the war on drugs. Here is a brief summary of the findings of that report: tens of thousands of children each year are becoming habituated to drugs (and notice how they grow up to be adult addicts); violent deaths, often involving innocent people, are occurring by the thousands every year as drug traffickers compete and law enforcement uses force to stop them; police officers and government officials in untold numbers corrupted by the temptations of sharing in the huge profits from sales to hard core users and addicts; and communities daily looted by the property crimes addicts commit when they can't otherwise feed their craving. Consider also the stress and tensions we suffer from the anger engendered in the minority communities where our drug policies are seen as racist and oppressive.

These problems, in one or more ways affect every living American. The history of our pursuit of prohibition has progressed with ill-advised and constitutionally questionable laws, all as has been documented by author Mike Gray, in his book *Drug Crazy*. And, the risks to the physical safety both for law breakers and innocent bystanders is well portrayed in Radley Balko's *Rise of the Warrior Cop*. And if you'd like a full grasp of the dark and ugly corruption that threatens the security in our communities and basic humanity in our prison systems, across the country, read Judge James Gray's book, *Why Our Drug Laws Have Failed and What We Can Do About It: A Judicial Indictment of the War on Drugs.*

Earnest origins

Society's concern with drug use and attempts to control it with prohibition go back only about a century. As with so many well-intentioned exercises of government power to change the vectors of human nature, this one was flawed from the start. The federal efforts at control began in 1914, with the Harrison Narcotics Act, which we rationalized as a tax measure, (to pass constitutional muster) aimed to suppress drugs including morphine, heroin, and cocaine.[22] For decades before the new law, doctors had been prescribing opiate medications, laudanum, morphine and more recently heroin for pain, but now were subject to federal arrest and jail time. For continuing to do so, the jaws of prison clamped down on thousands of physicians and surgeons doing their best for their patients.

The adoption of this act is an arresting study in political and social engineering. It was advanced under misconceptions and myths like those mentioned in the previous chapter.[23] There was very little in the way of any real drug related social problems early in the 20th century, though a large number of people in the U.S., had become addicted to cocaine or opium through the use of cure-all "medicines" that had begun to be peddled in the previous century following the Civil War.[24] In fact drug consumption in the U.S., after spiking in the mid-1890s, was on a steady decline by 1914.[25] The beginning of the new century was the period of Teddy Roosevelt progressivism. Reform was in the air. The calls for drug use regulation were amplified in this atmosphere. Restrictions were welcomed also because of racial prejudice against the Chinese and the Mexican immigrants. Some Chinese enjoyed opium, while some Mexicans enjoyed marijuana. The Act required anyone manufacturing, selling or giving away opiates or coca, or in possession of these drugs to register with the U.S. Treasurer and pay a tax. Violations of this law could get you 5 years in jail and a fine of $2,000, and, for many did.

At the time of passage of the law it was believed in Congress that drug addiction was easily cured. This belief appears to have been initiated by the unscientific claims of a sleazoid who promoted a cure for all forms of addiction.[26] A gullible professor at Cornell University naively authenticated the man's claims for a time. Those claims would be discredited, but not before they had cascaded through Washington as an important scientific breakthrough. In passing the law, Congress reasoned that though it would make instant law violators of tens of thousands of respectable middle-class folks addicted to patent medicines, those unfortunates could easily obtain a cure and cease their drug use. By the time the truth became known, we had a law and a public bias against the "evils" of narcotic drug use.[27] We also had the beginnings of a large black market that would eventually grow to its vast present-day dimensions.

In the meantime, the states were busy adopting their own laws against drugs. Marijuana was added to the list of outlawed drugs in 1937. The Nixon era term "war on drugs" originated in 1970 with the Controlled Substances Act, which was accompanied by legislation prescribing long prison terms for possession and trafficking in the scheduled drugs, and the virtual militarization of the Drug Enforcement Agency. By then the black market in drugs was a multi-billion-dollar industry and, despite the "war" rhetoric, since then has continued to grow and flourish.

We had been warned of this. In his 1936 book, *The Police and Modern Society*, former police chief and university professor, August Vollmer wrote:

> Stringent laws, spectacular police drives, vigorous prosecution, and imprisonment of addicts and peddlers have proved not only useless and enormously expensive as means of correcting this evil, but they are also unjustifiably and unbelievably cruel in their application to the unfortunate drug victims. Repression has driven this vice underground and produced the narcotic smugglers and supply agents, who have grown wealthy out of this evil practice and who by devious methods have stimulated traffic in drugs. Finally, and not the least of the evils associated with repression, the helpless addict has been forced to resort to crime in order to get money for the drug which is absolutely indispensable for his comfortable existence.[28]

Washington gets it wrong, again and again.

Despite the best of intentions, at least on the part of many of our policy makers, the "war on drugs" lost battle after battle. An expensive part of this war has been fought in Central and South

America. The federal government has spent billions on the attempt to induce farmers of coca to switch to ordinary commercial crops of fruit and vegetables. Bureaucrats who failed to consider the economic realities of the Andean farmers were frustrated. Even those farmers who attempted to switch soon found out they could not economically get their produce to market. Transportation expense, taxes, and spoilage in transit destroyed profits. With coca leaves turned into coca paste on the farm, the farmer had merely to wait for a FARC helicopter to land with bales of cash for which he could dispose of his produce and enjoy a good life. FARC is the paramilitary organization that has terrorized Columbia for decades and makes both drugs and money available to other terrorist organizations around the world. The farmers who had tried to cooperate gave up and switched back to supplying FARC. It is safer and more profitable. The Washington bureaucrats next tried sending in armies of men with chain saws to cut down the coca fields, but soon discovered the impossibility of making even a dent in the vast and widely distributed acreages of the fast-growing coca plants across the continent. Then aerial spraying with Agent Orange to kill off the coca fields, was proposed, but this was quickly shot down by the various governments as environmentally hazardous to flora, fauna and man, which of course it was.[29] For a time we tried spraying with glyphosate—brand name: Roundup— but that too has been stopped for environmental reasons.

Military style missions have been flown in to the area to interrupt and interdict the commerce of the well-equipped and well-armed traffickers working for the kingpins whose riches challenge the imagination. Costly and dangerous, this approach also failed to stanch the flow of cocaine and marijuana to North America.[30] For example, cocaine production in Bolivia has been on the increase since 2006 and that crime ridden country, while continuing to send it up through Mexico, has now kicked out the U.S. DEA.[31] In addition as has been widely reported, the U.S. trains Mexican military personnel in interdiction and capture techniques at considerable expense to the taxpayers. Success in high profile detentions of cartel kingpins, however, has failed to seriously dent their widely franchised operations which go on unabated.[32]

To this day we continue to try to induce the farmers to switch to licit crops, at gargantuan taxpayer expense, despite the absence of any substantial results to show for it.

Nixon's "war" produced a massive Drug Enforcement Agency (DEA), which itself is a bit of a boondoggle. The agency does garner media praise for huge interdictions at sea and on our borders, along with the vocal praise of politicians. And we read of multi-million-dollar confiscations at drop points inside the country. Even many DEA agents believe they are doing the Lord's work assuming each interdiction means shrinkage of supply headed to our streets.

Yet, taking a closer look, we find much more to the story. When we nab the smuggled inventory, the traffickers simply buy more from the farmers. The farmers have no power to raise prices and so they sell for a pittance the products that bring vast riches to the cartels. Farm gate prices, whether for opium, heroin or cocaine are a minor part of the costs of doing business. Moreover, the DEA is lucky to get 30% of the smuggled product. This pitiful yield on the money spent, led one former DEA officer to remark: "The war on drugs is a fucking lie." His point was that Americans read the headlines and assume we are doing serious damage to the drug trade. In fact, the massive supply is barely dented. For every 20-year-old he arrested for trafficking, two more popped up to take his place.[33]

Thousands of 18-wheelers cross from Mexico into the U.S. every day. Inspecting such huge cargo carriers is impossible without clogging the highways and stymying the flow of legitimate products into the U.S. Drugs also enter through our air ports and sea ports. The U.S. can't keep drugs out of our jails. Much more difficult is preventing them from coming through the entry points of our porous borders. Consider, for example, the great Mississippi River, a major transport artery from the Gulf of Mexico at New Orleans running north nearly to Chicago. Cargo barges as big as trucks, often linked in clusters of a couple dozen at a time, are powered up stream by pusher boats to moorings all along the way. Finding a few hundred pounds of heroin in all that tonnage would compare with finding that oft abused needle in a haystack.

Meanwhile despite President Obama's stated intentions to resort to a more health care based approach, with less emphasis upon criminal justice, we have not yet seen evidence of a meaningful change in policy.

In a 2017 evaluation of the U.K. governments enforcement policies, the findings included this unsurprising admission: "Activity solely to remove drugs from the market, for example, drug seizures, has little impact on availability." The report in a later passage admits: "There is, in general, a lack of robust evidence as to whether capture and punishment serves as a deterrent for drug use." And, "There is very limited evidence of the impact of stop and search on restricting supply."[34]

The federal prison population is the largest of any country in the world. It has grown nearly 800% since 1980 and houses nearly 219,000 inmates, about half of whom are there on drug crimes.[35]

State prisons house 5 or 6 times that many. Yet as noted above, we are spending a hundred billion dollars each year—a trillion in ten—with nothing meaningful to show for it.

Addiction is highly resistant to threats of punishment.

As we discuss below, our criminal justice system, a key tactical element in our war on drugs consistently fails to curb the demand that fuels the black market for drugs. Our laws and punishments are tougher than most other countries of relevant comparison, yet our per capita consumption is higher than 22 out of the 25 with which we can be compared.[36]

Severity of punishment does not predict use reduction by hard core users and addicts, as China has discovered. A country where drug *dealing* is punished with death, China's approach to control drug *using* is more extreme than ours. China makes drug addicts the enemy of the government as Zhang Wenjun learned. He was sent to detention centers and labor camps six times and six times tolerated the horrors of these detentions for the sake of his craving. Zhang now operates an organization that helps recovering addicts. He says 98 percent of those who are discharged from the drug detention system will suffer a relapse thereafter. How bad are these detention centers? Han Wei described his two-year experience: he said the guards would use electric prods on any who were less than cooperative. "At least they'd give us helmets so we wouldn't injure our heads during convulsions," he said. Meals consisted of steamed buns and, occasionally, cabbage-based swill. Showers were allowed once a month. And the treatment given for heroin withdrawal symptoms was a pail of cold water in the face. "They didn't give me a single pill or a bit of counseling." [37]

And, as mentioned above, the 2017 evaluation of enforcement policy in the U.K. admitted the absence of solid evidence that capture and punishment serve to deter drug use.[38]

The fact that the criminalization of drug use in this and other countries has not produced a substantial reduction in the demand for drugs, while countries with more liberal policies have seen lower drug consumption rates, has surprised many prohibitionists. And it has also become too apparent to be ignored. When Sweden adopted its zero-tolerance policy drug use did not diminish it increased.

True it is, that the U.S. saw a significant drop in drug use following President Nixon's "war on drugs" in 1971. Yet it is difficult to credit that drop to the anti-drug laws. Certainly, some quit or declined to start using because of the stringent criminal penalties. But, I am old enough to remember those days. The baby boomer generation, possibly the largest generation in American history, began to reach military draft age as the Vietnam war was in full swing. This young and affluent generation, so opposed to bearing the risks of fighting and dying in such a remote place, they took to the streets in huge numbers to protest it. At nearly the same time the hippie movement began and a new music form, called "rock 'n roll," supplied sounds in harmony with protest. Rebellion and protest was the cultural leading edge of the "boomer" generation. It was the era of the Timothy Leary types who encouraged teens and college partiers to "Turn on, tune in and drop out". A popular drug was LSD with its hallucinatory effects that some of our naïfs thought could lead to a spiritual and creative awakening. Smoking pot was a fun way to rebel. Joining street demonstrations was an easy way to get connected as protesters felt common bonds with one another. Partying with drugs was a favorite way both to rebel against authority and to find new hookups. Drug use rose from the late sixties into the early seventies.

By 1973, the Vietnam war was winding down and the draft ended and Leary was repeatedly jailed. As the decade matured drug use began to lessen and in the 80's and 90's as the boomers were now getting jobs and starting families drug use continued a downward trend. However, by the end of the century an upward trend was again in place and continued through the first decade of the new century. Over the ten years from 1998 to 2008, global consumption of illicit drugs increased dramatically – opiate use up 34.5%, cocaine up 27%, and cannabis up 8.5%. In the United States after the temporary drop, illicit drug use of all types zoomed back up to 7% of the population by 2010.

It is clear our pursuit of prohibition cannot claim any significant use reduction. In 2012, the United States Drug Use and Health (USDUH), published its survey results commonly called SAMHSA. Its table: "Types of Illicit Drug Use in Lifetime, Past Year, and Past Month among Persons Aged 12 or Older," showed about the same rates as for 2010 occurred in 2011: 14.9 % used in the previous year and 8.7 % used during the past month. Both years were higher than the 8.3% of 2003 and in both years the number of users was about 22.5 million, or about 7% of Americans of all ages. Today (2017) the estimate is 27 million total current users of illegal drugs.[39]

Still the simple fact is we are not a nation looking to get high. Treatment specialist Sally Satel, M.D., states: "On the whole, patients with chronic pain are more apt to underuse the narcotics that their physician prescribes than to abuse them."[40] Most people live comfortable lives with which getting high on drugs would interfere. Alcohol use is widespread, but those who abuse it are a small minority. Most use it for relaxation or stress relief—not to get high. And in a later chapter we will see how thousands of returning Vietnam veterans addicted to heroin, simply quit on returning home. They had families to think about and the world of work to enter.

It is sometimes said by those favoring prohibition that the prevention of one teenager from taking up illicit drug use justifies our current criminal punishment approach to deterrence. This is a noble sentiment, but far more teenagers are put at risk of drug use and addiction by the thriving underworld drug trade created by our pursuit of prohibition. Until we adopt a carefully controlled adult drug dispensary system, all teenagers will remain at risk.

As noted in the Report of the Global Commission (June 2011), "drug policies were initially developed and implemented in the hope of achieving outcomes in terms of a reduction in harms to individuals and society – less crime, better health, and more economic and social development." But, the report concluded:

> The global war on drugs has failed, with devastating consequences for individuals and societies around the world. Fifty years after the initiation of the UN Single Convention on Narcotic Drugs, and 40 years after President Nixon launched the US government's war on drugs, *fundamental* reforms in national and global drug control policies are *urgently* needed."[41] (Emphasis added)

The Global Commission consisted of prominent leaders from around the world. Some of them will be familiar to the reader. In the United States, most would recognize the names George Schulz, Paul Volcker, Kofi Annan, internationally respected author Mario Llosa, and; former president of Mexico, Ernesto Zedillo. There is no single political philosophy among these leaders. Schultz and Llosa are conservatives. Volker, an economist served as Chair of the Federal Reserve Board under both Presidents Carter and Reagan, earning the high regard of both presidents. Kofi Annan, former UN chief, is associated with the left as are some others on the Commission. The need for change is not a left versus right proposition. It is a simple, practical reality recognizable to all regardless of political ideology. So famous public intellectual William F. Buckley of PBS's "Firing Line" fame argued energetically. Buckley was considered by some as the "father of conservatism."

Violent consequences outside our borders of U.S. demand for drugs

While our government officials posture with words (for example President Obama's drug czar boasts: "a fundamental shift in the way we discuss this issue"), Mexico is suffering the devastating consequences of the demand for drugs in the U.S. There, just below the border and frequently above it, the drug cartels wage their internecine wars and orchestrate their accumulation of wealth and the resources that clear the way for their trafficking. More than 60,000 deaths, innocent bystanders as well as persons who pose a threat to a cartel's sway, were recorded during the six-year term of President Calderón, ending in 2012 and have continued at about the same rate ever since.

President Calderón sent the army to dozens of Mexican states to smack down the cartels and gangs fighting turf wars over lucrative drug-smuggling routes to the U.S. These efforts did not result in a significant reduction.[42] In 2017, news reports showed a continuation of the problem with over 20,000 deaths in 2015 alone. The drug cartels are still killing Mexican mayors and police chiefs, law enforcement personnel, journalists who fail to cooperate, competing traffickers, and anyone else who happens to get in the way.

It is the strong demand in the North American market, the U.S. and Canada, that provides the incentive to the Mexican and South American traffickers responsible for these murders.

As principal contributors to this problem the U.S. and Canada have accepted the responsibility to act toward disrupting the black-market operations and have made huge efforts to do so. We have interdicted great quantities of illegal drugs, jailed thousands of traffickers and dealers, closed hundreds of illegal labs, and incarcerated millions of drug offenders. We spend billions annually on these endeavors. Effects on drug consumption? Imperceptible.

The harms of imprisonment far outweigh the gains

A premise of our war on drugs is that the threat of imprisonment will deter the patronizing of the black-market traffickers and dealers. There is little doubt that the fear of detection and punishment will deter *some* young people who might otherwise experiment with drugs. So argue noted expert Mark Kleiman and his co-authors.[43] Still, as noted before, the evidence of actual drug use reduction due to punishment is weak at best.

While teens under 18 may only go to Juvenile Hall for drug use, older teens and young adults jailed for drug use are placed in close proximity to many practiced criminals from whom attitudes and methods are learned. Prisons have been called "crime schools., for good reason. Then too, the education and work careers of those jailed are detrimentally interrupted, a set-back with long term implications. A criminal record can follow, haunt and hamper them in the world of work, and diminish their aspirational opportunities and so their aspirations. When those sent to prison leave children behind the sociological consequences can be horrendous. The psychological/developmental damage done to a child whose parents, one or both, are jailed for their use results for many in that resentment and sense of deprivation that in their minds justifies crime and drug use.

A child whose mother is taken to prison suffers the loss of important nurturing that a working dad may not be able to supply. Women made up about 6% of the prison population in 2005, up 200% from 1978 according to Husak.[44] Tens of thousands of women are in prison on drug related offenses and 75% of them are single parents of young children.[45]

Data collected by government and private institutions explode two myths: 1) that drug use is primarily a problem among minority groups or sub-cultures with non-conventional moral systems, and 2) drug use is so debilitating to a normal person that an addict cannot be a contributing member of society and so may as well be institutionalized. In fact, drugs are used by law abiding and productive citizens of all ethnicities: blacks, whites, Hispanics and to a small extent Asians. Drug use is probably not a wise choice for many, but as we discuss later, we cannot conclude it necessarily leads adults into degenerate lives or that more than a small minority of them present a danger to themselves or others in society. Nevertheless, all drug users whether they are the many who exhibit few problems, or the few who do, are at risk of landing in jail if caught using.

Punishment by imprisonment presents terrible risks for the inmate. Most imprisoned for drug offenses are young men, though the gentler sex is not far behind. The young male sent to prison is exposed to the risk that sometimes materializes: the horror of rape and the disaster of HIV/aids infection. Judge Gray, in his book, quotes a New York Times article by Chief Judge Donald P. Lay of the Court of Appeals for the Eighth district who said that the atrocities that take place within prisons are common place. He tells of a young man sentenced to a year in prison for marijuana possession. The prison was grossly over-populated. The fellow was locked in with 11 cellmates and was raped several dozen times over a 48-hour period.[46] Women inmates, too, may be sexually assaulted both homosexually, and by male guards. Guards are not angels, and they command a position of power over inmates, eager to please and earn a favorable behavior report. Some states distribute condoms to all inmates to reduce sexually transmitted disease through unwanted as well as consensual sex. The risk of prison rape has been recognized by federal authorities and steps have been taken to curtail it. In 2012, the Department of Justice issued its "final rule to prevent, detect and respond to sexual abuse in confinement facilities, in accordance with the Prison Rape Elimination Act of 2003 (PREA)." Whether such a "final rule" will be sufficient to stop this evil, where previous rules had not been, is still an open question.

As we discuss in Chapter 3, drug court programs have been a positive development and help to reduce the risks to those convicted by offering them probation rather than prison. It is rare today that first time offenders go to jail and even repeat offenders often receive a probationary chance to stop using. Still many are jailed on drug law violations. According to Gil Kerlikowske, President Obama's Drug Czar, "In 2011, about seven million people were under the supervision of the state and federal criminal justice systems in the United States. Of these, about two million were behind bars. And nearly one quarter - 500,000 - of those behind bars are there for drug related offenses."[47]

More recently the Obama administration adopted a policy of early release for many non-violent offenders, including drug offenders, but the number of state and federal prisoners remains little changed.

Allow me to digress briefly to note a related fact here. Those seven million under state and federal justice system supervision were involved with various crimes, not just drug crimes. Five of those seven million were not in jail, but on probation. If a quarter of all offenders were involved with drugs, it means only about 1.25 million drug users are under drug court supervision, i.e., on probation. (.25X5,000,000) In a later chapter we will discuss whether drug courts are helping with drug addiction. According to SAMHSA, about 7.1 million have "substance use disorders." Thus, by a huge majority, troubled users are not being helped by drug courts.

We also noted above that about 17% of prisoners committed their crime to finance their drug purchases. That's about 340,000 men and women. Petty theft, prostitution and small-scale drug dealing are common. Many commit multiple offenses per day for this purpose. This reality affects community health and safety and reveals a system that is not working very well, if at all. One of the most widely remarked and documented consequences of the higher prices engendered by the drug war is the reality of property crimes committed to finance a drug habit.

In remarks at the Annual Meeting of the American Bar Association's House of Delegates, August 12, 2013, Attorney General Eric Holder among other things said:

> As the so-called "war on drugs" enters its fifth decade, we need to ask whether it, and the approaches that comprise it, have been truly effective – and build on the

Administration's efforts, led by the Office of National Drug Control Policy, to usher in a new approach. And with an outsized, unnecessarily large prison population, we need to ensure that incarceration is used to punish, deter, and rehabilitate – not merely to warehouse and forget. Today, a vicious cycle of poverty, criminality, and incarceration traps too many Americans and weakens too many communities. And many aspects of our criminal justice system may actually exacerbate these problems, rather than alleviate them.

What was that? Prison might make matters worse, not better? This proposition is well researched and proved. A prison term leads to "statistical discrimination" a scholar's term, referring to the fact that a convict, especially a minority person, may have his chances for employment reduced to near zero.[48] A life of crime including drug use and dealing may in those circumstances be attractive. For the addict, a feedback loop develops as the individual is convicted for a drug offense, then upon release cannot get work, craves drugs enough to commit more crime to buy them, is then arrested again, and the cycle repeats. Tens of thousands ride this sad merry-go-round each year.

The death and disease by-products of prohibition

The stigma and inhumanity of imprisonment are not the only devastating consequences of jailing people with substance use disorders. Americans in our "land of the free" are also increasingly subjected to the terror of aggressive police action gone wrong. Stories abound of erroneous targeting by police of people whose only crime is possession of a small amount of an illegal drug and people innocent of any wrongdoing at all. Dismissal of charges following arrest and a night in jail is little solace for the fear and rough treatment to which an arrestee is sometimes subjected. A civil suit vindication does not make a family whole for the pointless loss of a loved one. The increased militarization of our police forces across the country has been well-documented.[49]

Appearing in the *Journal of the American Medical Association* is a discussion of deaths in the U.S. in each of the years 1990 and 2000. Illicit drug dealing and use were responsible in the U.S. for 20,000 deaths in 1990 and 17,000 deaths in 2000—a drop consistent with the temporary drop in drug usage over that period. Since then drug use has regained its highs.[50] Today doctors speak of the epidemic of drug overdose and death—33,000 opioid overdose deaths in the single year 2015,[51] with no evidence of slowing since.

Gangster violence causes thousands of deaths each year as gangs compete in the drug market. There exist wide variations in such death rates from city to city, but the risks to community security and health are obvious. Most street gangs would be pathetically feeble without drug sales and profits. Those profits are what hold them together and they protect their businesses by violent means. Innocent bystanders are often injured or killed. One vivid example tells of a drug dealer who drove to a Colombian owned store in Florida and in anger at a competitor machine gunned everyone in sight. Though violence is more prevalent in Mexico and South America, drug dealer violence in America has become a major problem as the Mexican traffickers try to move down the distribution chain to by-pass American dealers and sell direct to users. News reports of arrested drug dealers nearly always mention weapons in their possession, or in their homes or cars.

Clearly, we cannot say the pursuit of prohibition has made our communities safer. Some law enforcement experts have stated that because of it they have become less so.[52] Crack wars in Chicago in the 1980s and 1990s took the murder rate in that city to a high of 900 per year. That rate was reduced when an aggressive program to capture gang leaders was carried out.[53] Still the Chicago gang and violence rate, fueled by drug dealing, continues to produce several hundred deaths.

The Chicago gangs multiplied as an unintended consequence of city gentrification efforts to bring down blighted housing projects, where a few large gangs were holding sway. The smackdown of those gangs scattered numbers of small operators over a larger region where they claimed and began to defend separate territories. Even worse, individual operators and new smaller gangs ranged out into the suburbs, becoming even more accessible to minors. Some of these criminal operations are run by 15-year-olds.[54] Chicago's example is no outlier. Major cities all over America are similarly plagued by gangs and violence. There is no hopeful sign on the horizon that continuing to pursue prohibition will change this ugly picture and the costs in human life are enormous.

Violence of the illegal traffickers is not, however, the only violent by-product of our drug war. Over the past several decades there has been an increase in swat teams and in the shock and awe approach to drug raids on homes and businesses: what one author has called, with good reason, the militarization of the police.[55] Numerous examples of unjustified police violence show that in our zeal to stamp out drug dealing by force police agencies have escalated the use of money, men and materiel in methods posing immense risk to community safety. One story is of a raid on a home, where drugs were suspected, that went horribly wrong. A later investigation revealed there had been scant evidence to justify the raid. With all members of the Sepulveda family face down on the floor, the shotgun of one of the swat team members accidentally fired at close range to the head of an 11-year- old, killing him. The search turned up no drugs. The state of California paid the family $3 million in damages.[56] Not much for such a heartbreaking loss.

We should grieve too for the officers who must live out their lives with such memories of tragedies justified only by the enforcement of our dubious drug laws.

While we do not base policy on isolated and highly emotional stories such as the tragedy of the Sepulveda family's, it does illustrate the point that the police, even when trying to avoid injury to the innocent, are in the violence business. Community safety is compromised every time weapons are unsheathed as in search and seizure operations. The natural question begs an answer: even though incidents such as the killing of the Sepulveda boy are infrequent, can we justify taking such risks? Should we be less concerned for public safety in this context than in the context of workplace injuries where our occupational safety (OSHA) laws are detailed, pervasive and strictly enforced? Of course not.

Accidental police violence in the pursuit of illegal traffickers will likely continue under any system. But, what I propose is a system that will guarantee a reduction in the need for armed confrontations as the number of traffickers, dealers, user-dealers shrinks. Until the traffickers are defeated by the economic force of an adult use tolerant system that destroys their businesses, we will continue to be exposed to such risks to community safety.

The global supply and corruption created by drug demand in North America

The lucrative adult drug market in the U.S. and Canada is enormous and fuels much of the worldwide production and trafficking of drugs. The powerful and well-funded cartels have no problem getting their goods into the North American market.

Consider the following news story. In a gated community in the Sierra foothills an ostensibly respectable couple whom I shall fictitiously name Jack and Jill McGee made their home. From their home, the county airport is about sixteen miles away. There they maintained their privately-owned airplane. In 2012, they were sentenced in federal court in Sacramento, convicted of international drug smuggling and money laundering. During the investigation by the DEA and Homeland Security their home was searched and at least a dozen duffel bags bulging with over 400 pounds of marijuana were found. Also found were bundles of cash amounting to $316,000. Some of the cash bundles were in plain sight on the kitchen counter, as if they were of little more importance than the morning paper. The McGees were not merely engaged in the distribution of marijuana. According to the report they were part of a drug trafficking organization in the business of smuggling marijuana to various locales including Chicago, Detroit, St. Louis, Atlanta, Los Angeles and cities in Canada, and with the proceeds of those sales purchasing one to two hundred kilos of cocaine each month in Mexico. The cocaine was then being sold in the U.S. and Canada. This couple did well at this game. They owned two homes and two airport hangers, an airplane and a boat, among other nice things. Jack was not new to the trade. He had previously been arrested and convicted on drug sale charges. Yet thereafter he ranged free from detection for years, before he was stopped the second time.

In prison, the McGees cost the taxpayers of California $47,000 per year each during their stay there, while other dealers jump up to fill their niche and continue the supply chain from all over the world. They were operating more than four decades after our government declared a "war on drugs" and it is certainly not a one-off story. The multitude of such operators across the country supplies the many thousands of gangs and small-scale dealers who obtain inventory from them. The enormous profits at the wholesale level lured Jack McGee back into the game despite his earlier conviction. He was able, after resuming the trade to enjoy a standard of living few in America can afford. He got caught and that is a victory in one skirmish in the war on drugs. But, we know from experience there are plenty of others to take their place and that such traffickers continue to do business both after prison and sometimes direct their operations right from inside prison walls.

Methamphetamine has become a widely available and popular drug, too. It is highly profitable to the makers and dealers. It goes for $800 an ounce on the street, but few users can afford to buy such a quantity at one time and so it is parceled out in small packages of a gram or so each. Another true story reported in the press in 2013, was that of a meth dealer I fictitiously here call Eddie Dopedus. At age 33, Eddie was arrested for the third time in less than a year for possession of methamphetamine. In 2012, he had been found guilty of possession of two pounds of meth with a street value of over $25,000. He had struck a plea bargain with prosecutors on that charge by which he would go to prison for 2 years. While awaiting the court's sentencing order on that deal he was caught again in early 2013 with 2 ounces of meth with a street value of about $1,600. Still out on bail two months later he was caught a 3rd time with more than 3 ounces of meth. Meanwhile the DEA got involved and a federal grand jury issued a formal accusation. The potential federal punishment for his 2012 crime is a maximum fine of $5 Million or 40 years in prison, or both. Out on bail and undeterred even by the risk of such harsh punishment, Eddie had been going about his business selling meth. Such is the lure of drug dealing. For an informative portrayal of the meth trade see Scott Anderson's, book *Shadow People.*

These stories are of dealers who got caught. The massive size of the North American drug market attests to the many that do not get caught. Most dealers are small-scale operators such as Eddy, and gangs, few of whom make very much in the trade, but do it for the comparatively easy profit. Much of the drug dealing is done by users who have entered the business to finance their own habits. Much larger profits are made by the traffickers like Jack and Jill McGee working at the wholesale level, while even bigger profits are made by the cartels for which they distribute the drugs. Foreign production is cheap while the domestic supply, on offer through local sellers, commands prices sufficient to earn big money for a few—a bare living for the much more numerous small-scale dealers.

Drug prohibition has been promoted by some policy makers on the grounds it keeps illegal drug prices high. Yet it has failed to raise the street price of drugs to levels which retard demand. Illegal drug prices are well above prices at which legally manufactured drugs could be supplied, but the demand has remained inelastic—meaning users are willing to pay up.[57]Those who have turned to crime for drug money, just work a little harder than they would with lower prices.

Fifty-eight percent of world drug trafficking is aimed at North America.[58] Although the available data is limited, what information we do have suggests that 5% of the world's populations are users of illicit drugs,[59]compared to 7% in the U.S. Here the demand is for marijuana, heroin, cocaine, methamphetamine, Ecstasy, hallucinogens and, heroin substitutes such as oxycodone and fentanyl. By a wide margin the drugs most used are the opioids, the legally manufactured pain medication and their illegal imitators.[60] In addition, there are the designer drugs with unfamiliar chemical names which supplement or replace the other drugs.

The American Association of Poison Control Centers reported 6,138 calls were made in 2011, reporting abuse of the synthetics, up from 302 calls the year before, though in 2012, the number of calls dropped to 2,657. Chemists can tweak molecules in various compounds so they mimic the scheduled drugs in effect, but differ enough to make prosecution for illegal drug possession difficult.[61] Here, again, we see the power of economics in operation to the delight of the drug marketeers, a power we could take away from them in the System I propose.

Marijuana is grown massively in many parts of the world including in the United States. The raw materials for the other plant-based drugs are grown in parts of the world. Opium poppies are grown in Afghanistan, but also in Mexico which has become a major supplier. Coca is grown and refined into a precursor of cocaine in the Andean countries Venezuela, Columbia, Ecuador, and Chile where the climate also fosters growth of opium poppies and coca. Peasant farmers are motivated by what to them are high cash prices for these crops far surpassing vegetable crop prices.

In the last couple of decades poppy cultivation has grown in Mexico by leaps and bounds partly due to the popularity of black tar heroin. Black tar is made from the morphine extracted from the seed pod of the plant. It is a clay like product that can be pressed into the cavities in and around the component parts of products such as radios and computers to escape detection during transport. User's like it because it is pure heroin and cheaper than powder heroin. Small wads of it are packaged in tiny rubber balloons and runners carry a profitable supply in their mouths giving them the sobriquet "chipmunks."[62]

Extensive growth in the production of drugs for the North American and European markets continues despite the adoption of international agreements to ban them. It continues apparently unaffected by the United Nations drug treaties including its Single Convention on Narcotic Drugs in 1961, its Convention on Psychotropic Substances of 1971 and the UN Convention Against

Illicit Traffic in Narcotic Drugs and Psychotropic Substances of 1988. So ineffective have these international agreements been, one wonders if the strategy involves more than just stretching out their titles.

Drugs continue to flow into the U.S. in hundreds of tons every year. Well-equipped traffickers bring them to our seashores in small go-fast boats and through our coastal ports as well. Carriers of the contraband include not only the members of the crime organizations and members of their families as tourists, but also bribed and corrupt diplomats, pilots and other airline employees, professional athletes, traveling students, ship captains, and others. Drug profits are tempting. Heroin, begins at the "farm gate" for about $70 for a kilo or 2.2 pounds. The buyer turns can sell it there to other traffickers at about $5,000, but he'll get several times that in the U.S., where its street value will likely reach $80,000 and more. Cocaine is similarly profitable. The cartels in Mexico amass great wealth by selling inventory in the U.S. to the criminal gangs and the dealers large and small.

Coca paste refined from coca leaves grown in South America follows a similar pattern though its pricing is lower than opium and heroin. Our borders pose no serious obstacles to the sophisticated and well-funded operators who boast that they are able through a web of air, sea and land routes to bring cocaine into the U.S. safely any time they like. The McGee story above is a graphic example of common commerce.

The staggering humanity costs render the picture grotesque. Thanks to the profitability of drug trafficking, the violent Mexican cartels are well-armed, sophisticated in the ways of corruption and able to intimidate, bribe or confound Mexican officials to gain their cooperation. Competition among the Mexican and South American cartels in the drug trade is fierce. Even law enforcement officers are brazenly threatened with harm to their families if they refuse to accept a bribe and cooperate. It all goes on despite the aggressive, military style crack-down by the Mexican government aided by our DEA and military personnel. Decapitating a cartel, as when we apprehended the Sinaloa chief, El Chapo Guzman in 2016, does not reduce the trafficking activities of its members. It just scatters them to form smaller more widely spread operations. Turf wars among these profiteers are the bloody consequence.

As so we see that the devastation we live with is not only unfazed by our pursuit of prohibition, it is fostered by it. What are we doing about it? At least some of us are trying to reduce the harms of our laws. In the next chapter, we see the intelligent harm reduction efforts being made and how they point the way to a more comprehensive reform.

Chapter 3:

Harm Reduction Measures Offer Some Help, but....

Most of the harm that comes from drugs is because they are illegal

Milton Friedman

Over the past several decades as the worst consequences of drug prohibition have been observed, pressure has mounted steadily for the adoption of measures to reduce the harms to individuals, while maintaining a catch and cage approach to use reduction. We are learning a lot from these harm reduction measures. Among other things, though skeptics call it a back-door scheme to legalized drugs, they serve the cause of both use and addiction reduction. Our pursuit of prohibition is working against its own purposes.

Progress to date in "harm reduction," promising, but limited.

Use of the term "harm reduction" began around the time the Netherlands acted to deal with the problem that disease was spreading among users who inject their drugs. Addicts needing a fix to avoid the sickness of withdrawal are often keener to get the injection than to avoid the risk of a contaminated needle.   The government's provision of clean needles resulted in a dramatic reduction in the incidence of new HIV/Aids and Hepatitis C cases.

In the U.S. many communities are allowing clean needle exchanges to serve users of injectable drugs with similar results. Contrary to the claim it removes an incentive to quit drugs, there is no evidence it promotes continued use. The addicted user without access to a clean needle is nearly always willing to accept the risks of a used one.

Harm reduction is defined by the International Harm Reduction Association, an NGO claiming a membership of over 8,000, as follows:

> Harm Reduction refers to policies, programmes and practices that aim primarily to reduce the adverse health, social and economic consequences of the use of legal and illegal psychoactive drugs without necessarily reducing drug consumption. Harm reduction benefits people who use drugs, their families and the community.[63]

The concept, however praiseworthy, has so far advanced only sporadically in places where voters have welcomed them. In most parts of the U.S., the harms of drug prohibition continue unabated, despite the unmistakable evidence of their benefits wherever they have been accepted.

One of these programs, still controversial in the U.S., but accepted in dozens of cities around the world, is the supervised injection facility. (SIF). In 2003, based on the experience of European success in reducing overdose deaths and disease spread, the city of Vancouver in British Columbia established a partnership between the the city health agency and a non-profit care provider. Called Insite, it is a visibly public service for injection drug users. Use of the facility is free to users, who bring their own drugs and inject them with clean needles provided there, and in the presence of nurses, ready to act if necessary to reverse an overdose. Upstairs in the same building detox beds along with rehab services are available to addicts who want them. There, by 2016, over 4,000 have been referred to detox.[64]

Hard line prohibitionists sued to stop the operation and the issue had to be resolved in Canada's courts. Their Supreme Court found the evident success of the program justified the legal exemption the City had given it. Peer-reviewed studies published in reputable medical journals such as The Lancet, the New England Journal of Medicine, and the British Medical Journal, all have described Insite's effect in saving lives, reducing disease and promoting rehab positive and it enjoys the support of the Canadian Medical Association.[65]There has been no increase in drug use in the neighborhood while compared, with the rest of Vancouver, the program has dramatically reduced overdose death.[66]

And it likely reduces drug use. Insite refers hundreds of users to rehab each year. Of the 6,500 people who visited Insite in 2016,[67] 464 were referred to the detox center and rehab. Of those, 252 finished treatment. Studies have indicated there has not been any increased drug use in the area served by Insite or similar facilities in other countries. In Australia, Holland, Germany, Switzerland and Spain, where injection centers are allowed, huge public health and safety savings have been realized along with many successful referrals to treatment.[68] Problematic users, in relationships with care providers who show them a modicum of respect, develop a better self-identity and are better able to envision a different future.[69] As we'll show in Chapter 7, a renewed self-awareness is key to addiction recovery.

Injection facilities offer the lesson that bringing people into the fold of caring service providers promotes rehab and to that extent the reduction of use. [70]

Approvals to set up injection sites, are being sought in several cities in the U.S., and there is a strong movement to allow them. They provide solid evidence that we have little to fear and a lot to gain in saving lives. Addiction psychiatrist, Sally Satel, M.D. observed: "Drug-war weary police officers and harm reductionists would rather see addicts opt for treatment and lasting recovery, but they'll settle for fewer deaths."[71]

Toleration of adult drug use in the Netherlands and other countries such as Switzerland and Portugal have all resulted in a reduction of drug use. Contrast this with the experience of Sweden following its adoption of a zero-tolerance policy. Sweden began to experience an increase in drug use even as the Netherlands saw its drug use decline.

The Dutch Minister of Foreign Affairs, at a 2009 conference in Amsterdam said:

> The pragmatic approach that we have developed in the Netherlands didn't come about overnight.... It is based on a simple basic idea: drug addiction is (probably) first and foremost an illness. Only once we had accepted this fact could we implement a series of measures that combined to create a more dignified existence for those who, for whatever reason, were addicted to drugs.

The Dutch legal approach to drug control might be considered incoherent, but it is working. Their opium act of 1976 is still in force. It outlaws possession, production, and distribution of the enumerated hard drugs such as cocaine, heroin, and ecstasy, and deems these activities a criminal offense. Still they treat use of drugs as primarily a health issue, while keeping laws on the books which make it criminal to possess them, and law enforcement generally looks the other way. Use is not a criminal offense, but "possession" even for personal use is. The policy, however, is that small amounts possessed for personal use will simply be ignored. Cities and towns can set up injection sites where users can take their dose with a nurse nearby. Drug dealing near these rooms is forbidden. Cannabis products are openly sold in Holland. The "coffee shops" where Dutch citizens and foreigners alike can buy pot, are regulated, but allowed to sell "soft drugs" including marijuana, hashish and other cannabis products.

Similar decriminalization of possession and use in Portugal has reduced the illegal use among teens, the exact opposite of what had been feared by the prohibitionists, and a paper published by the Cato Institute in 2009 commented: "Judging by every metric, decriminalization in Portugal has been a resounding success."[72] Later investigations have borne that out, especially as users have become willing to discuss their problems with social workers.[73]

In 2009 the people of Switzerland voted to adopt nationwide the policy experiment first tried by one of its 26 Cantons. The new policy treats most drug use or possession offenses as administrative infractions subject to fines rather than incarceration. This approach was felt by most of the Swiss to be consistent with their four-pillar policy: prevention, therapy, harm reduction and prohibition. This policy is based upon a decade of experience–and success–with heroin and methadone treatment programs provided by the government, plus the reductions they achieved in HIV/ Aids and hepatitis C transmission through clean needle provision. Doctors saw that the harms of drug injection could be controlled more effectively by public health programs than by policing, and became active in the drive to change Swiss policy from prohibition to a set of alternatives promoting wellness.

These changes in Switzerland came with a good deal of political opposition by people fearing a slippery slope toward acceptance of harmful drugs as social norm. That is a rational concern, but, like Switzerland, country after country has shown it does not happen. A use tolerant system, such as I propose, would reduce the government role to one of regulating a controlled dispensation of safe drugs to adults, while making them unavailable to minors. It would preserve prohibition of purchase from illicit traffickers and dealers, while permitting adult users to move toward freedom from drugs at their own pace and in a way that works best for them.

Another more recent law enforcement approach fits the harm reduction concept. The LEAD program was initiated in Seattle and followed in several other U.S. cities. It stands for law enforcement administrative diversion. Instead of being taken into court, low-level drug offenders are offered the option of cooperating in a counseling program. In collaboration with a non-profit provider, the policy diverts arrestees into a program that helps them stabilize their lives with housing, medical care and even employment assistance. The program gives them a chance to clean up their acts and learn more about how to get free from the addiction trap. Seattle pays several hundred thousand dollars to the non-profit administering the program, but has found it so improves neighborhoods, it saves even more dollars in policing costs and in dealing with health and social issues. A helping hand works better than the catch and cage idea of criminal law. While abstinence is nominally required, the program does not give up on those who occasionally relapse briefly.

Another form of harm reduction in some communities involves follow up visits with overdose emergencies by police after the patients return home. Officers engage them in discussions about treatment options. Some city ordinances allow drug users to walk into the police station, hand over their drugs and enter treatment without arrest or charges. And, of course, clean needle/syringe exchanges all over the country are helping to reduce disease spread.

Drug courts help to reduce harms, but impact too few.

Drug courts are not generally thought of in the harm reduction context, but the inhumanity of jailing ordinary users and the damage it does to employment and educational opportunities and family integrity are certainly among the reasons for developing them.

Most if not all the States have some form of drug court program underway and these may take two forms – one specializing in the handling of non-violent drug offenders, and dealing with the rest. California is such a state. Its "Prop 36" drug courts are for *non-violent* offenders who are convicted of being under the influence of a controlled substance, or in possession of or of transporting same. These folks are placed on probation. A condition of that probation is that the defendants initiate and follow through on a treatment plan. If they violate probation by using or failing to follow through with treatment they are brought back into court, where measures such as increasing supervision and the supervision fee they must pay, among other measures, are employed to discourage further violations. Repeated violations mean jail time. Upon successful completion of the program the defendant is discharged and his arrest and conviction are deemed never to have occurred.

The other form of drug court–the adult criminal drug court–is employed in all states. This jurisdiction differs from Prop 36 type courts in that the defendant has been convicted of a serious crime and violation of probation may return him promptly to prison. Also, these people do not automatically qualify for participation. Typically, they get a psychiatric examination to determine if they are suitable candidates, likely able to comply with the conditions of a probationary period. A standard condition of admission also is that the defendant is one who is subject to a long-term prison sentence. Those expected to be released in short order do not usually qualify as there would be little incentive on the defendant's part to cooperate.   If allowed into the program these people are treated with dignity and caring while they proceed in treatment under probationary supervision and periodic random testing. Graduates of this program are honored with a graduation day celebration in the presence of their drug court colleagues.

Drug courts have succeeded in reducing enforcement costs. A 2008 study at U.C.L.A. of California's Prop 36 program is illustrative. During the year ending June 30, 2006, the program's fifth year in operation, over fifty thousand offenders were referred for treatment and of that number 71.4% entered treatment. Most of the treatment clients were non-Hispanic whites, while a third were Hispanic and about 14% were black. The average age of admittees was thirty-five. For more than half, methamphetamine was the primary drug followed by cocaine and marijuana at about 13%, each with alcohol and heroin at about 8% each. Cost savings were substantial at nearly $2,000 per offender, which meant a ratio of $2 saved for every $1 invested.

The National Association of Drug Court Professionals (NADCP) states there are 1.2 million addicts nationwide under drug court supervision.[74] That's a small subset of the addicted population. SAMHSA now estimates there are 27 million users in the U.S. with about 7.1 who have illicit substance use disorders. Since drug courts are dealing with only a fraction of the users their impact is limited—the clear majority are not being seen in these courts. Still for those in the system they help. The NADCP states that 75% of drug court graduates do not recidivate within the two years following graduation. Probationers who do not complete their programs show rates of recidivism of about 40%.[75]

A separate issue relating to the efficacy of drug court success with addicts has been raised by critics of the 12-Step approach to treatment.[76] The 12-Step method of AA and NA is the dominant choice in drug court referrals as shown by journalist Ann Fletcher who refers to the approach as "one size fits all." [77] Later we discuss the importance of patient motivation to successful recovery. One aspect of the weakness of 12 Step mentioned by numerous authors is illustrated by the case, known personally to me, of a young man I fictitiously name Hal. A bright, if impulsive, teenager in California he used methamphetamine for several years before he was first arrested in his early 20's. The Drug Court sent him to an AA group for treatment. There he was told that he would need to surrender himself to a higher power without which he was helpless and that he was destined to be a drug addict the rest of his life. His only hope was that he might learn to stay sober. He refused to accept this posture of helplessness and dependence upon a "higher power" and was ousted from the group when he showed lack of commitment to its methods. He was bounced back to court and sentenced to jail. Hal expresses a low opinion of the group he attended and its leader, a felony convict, whom Hal said lacked needed skills for this role. This problem was also observed by journalist Maia Szalavitz, whose experience not only included incompetent leaders, but some who are sexually predatory as well.[78]

Many 12 Step groups are led by those whose only "training" is that they have completed the steps. Fletcher also argues that the greater number of available treatment programs, many of which are very expensive, mostly use one size fits all approaches, often led by less than well trained or properly motivated people.[79] Hal eventually proved the point that, contrary to the teachings of 12-Step, addicts can recover on their own; they do not need to think of themselves as helpless, lifetime addicts. Over the years Hal saw the unmistakable connection between his loss of jobs and the alienation of family and friends. These painful consequences of his drug use motivated him to quit and he succeeded at age 39. He has been dug free for over seven years.

A principle argument for drug courts is that the threat of jail provides an incentive for the addicted to quit. This argument has merit. But, while this incentive is effective for some addicts, other incentives are just as effective. All addicts eventually reach a point they don't want to be that way anymore. Many, like Hal, quit on their own, without treatment,[80] and no doubt, like Hal, many prolong the problem by putting off quitting in hopes of some new medical cure that never materialized.[81] And, those who need or choose rehab treatment face a confusing array of alternative programs. The widespread lack of treatment information keeps many addicts in a struggling and failing pattern. The System proposed here would not allow ignorance of these sorts to continue.

New York's Special Narcotics Prosecutor describes their drug court program:

> For addicted criminal offenders, an effective drug treatment program can mean the difference between repeated terms of imprisonment and the ability to lead a productive, law-abiding life. Yet it is not enough to simply conquer addiction. To begin anew, recovering drug users require skills gained through academic and vocational training, along with supportive counseling.

> ... highly experienced staff members evaluate offenders to identify those who are likely to reap the benefits of treatment. Eligible candidates are given the opportunity to enter an appropriate program, most often at a long-term residential facility, instead of going to prison. Beginning

in October 2009, new legislation allowed judges to place defendants in court-sponsored diversion programs.

… Upon successful completion, charges may be dismissed. If an offender fails to abide by the rules of a program, they face a sanction. If they commit a new crime, their original prison sentence may be imposed. Since the inception of the division, more than 2,000 offenders have been placed into treatment.

These approaches and the trends they demonstrate are a result of state governors and legislatures looking with alarm at prison costs eating up increasing shares of their budgets as well as the inhumanity and counterproductive effects of incarcerating drug users. According to Adam Gelb, director of the Public Safety Performance Project for the Pew Center, more than half the states and the District are trying to reduce the growth in their prison populations through alternative sentencing and through new probation and parole procedures. '"The economy is bringing a lot of states to the table," Gelb said, "and the research has pointed to a path for them to more public safety at less cost."[82] The cost savings are obvious and measurable. Quoting Gelb again: "According to Pew, it costs an average of \$79 a day to keep an inmate in prison but about \$3.50 a day to monitor the same person on probation or parole."' [83]

While we can applaud the positive development of all these measures, we are still faced with a major problem: they cannot address the ever-present lure of black market drugs so easily accessed by the very young as well as adults. The drug arrestees, who do not receive an alternative sentence diversion to probation, most often do their time and return to that market again for drugs. Those who are given probation are still subject to that same lure and many will violate probation and patronize the traffickers and dealers. Even those who successfully graduate from drug court and stay clean for lengthy periods may still have whatever vulnerability responsible for their addiction in the first place. And, of course, most drug users never see a drug court.

Chapter 4:

Why Not Just Legalize Drugs for Adults?

You wanna get rid of drug crime in this country? Fine, let's just get rid of all the drug laws.

Ron Paul

There are many strong voices in favor of legalizing drugs, or in the alternative, decriminalizing their possession and use. One is that of the highly regarded former police chief and Hoover Institute Fellow Joseph McNamara who put it this way:

…the prohibition of drugs is worse than the problem was. And that's why I've worked with LEAP for so many years, the Law Enforcement Against Prohibition, because it's people on the front line, more and more, that begin to realize that what we are doing actually, as we try to enforce these laws, is creating more violence, more corruption and, actually more drug use because we've generated this vast illegal market which is probably one of the biggest, if not the biggest market in the world's economy.[84]

The late Chief McNamara's reputation as a visionary police chief took on near iconic proportions while serving first as Chief for Kansas City, MO, and then San Jose, CA. Skeptics will suggest he reflected the progressive ideology typical of California, but he was in fact a conservative and spent many of his later years as a scholar at the conservative think tank, the Hoover Institute. It is the thinking of people like McNamara we need to inform our drug policy.

His supports one of the central observations of this book: the laws against drugs are promoting more use not less by fostering a huge illegal market. Not mentioned in the above quote is that it is the illegal market that makes drugs available to minors, where over 90% of substance use disorders form. Ponder this for a moment. Nine in ten adult addicts got their start on drugs as teenagers. Destroy the black market in drugs and you can do something about that.

Why then do we not just shut down this failed war on drugs, legalize drug use for adults, and like cigarettes and alcohol just ban sales to minors? Later, I will review the more salient arguments for legalization as they lend support for the *toleration feature* of the System I propose—and lay out the salient arguments against legalization as it supports the *control features* of the System I propose. But, first we examine decriminalization.

Decriminalization: the incoherent compromise

The word "decriminalization" differs from legalization. It represents a system in which drug use remains illegal, but punishment is waived for possession of small amounts. When users are caught they just get a ticket, similar to a traffic ticket, with some sort of "drugs are bad for you" counseling. But, notice another significant difference from legalization: under decriminalization the illegal traffickers continue to ply their trade and to protect their businesses with violence and corruption, and the small-scale dealers and user/dealers continue to operate in and near schools where minors access them. Users continue to depend on supplies of drugs often tainted with additives, sometimes dangerous to health. Decriminalization would be far more humane than prison terms for the addicted, but it would do nothing to solve the important problem of protecting against adolescent experimentation. It does nothing to reduce crime committed to buy drugs or illegal drug dealing, with all its associated corruption and violence. Users would continue to buy sometimes tainted drugs, and inject unsafely with dirty needles. Some users would continue to prostitute themselves in exchange for drugs and community health would continue to be plagued with addiction at current levels.

The Portuguese solution

Risking a loss of respect for law among its people, Portugal began an experiment in 2001 with its own version of decriminalization. Possession of small amounts of cannabis, heroin or cocaine was reduced from an indictable felony offense to a misdemeanor—one with practically no punishment. Other drugs such as ecstasy and methamphetamine are also allowed. The quantity with which one can stroll down Lisbon's Avenida da Liberdade amounts to about a 10-day supply. This means that you will not be arrested for carrying a single gram of heroin, two grams of cocaine, 25 grams of marijuana leaves or five grams of hashish. If suspected by the police of possessing drugs you can be stopped, searched, and if you have too much, arrested as a drug dealer. The police weigh your stash to see if it's within the legal limits. If it is, your worst-case scenario is you must report to the warning commission on drug addiction within 72 hours. There you are interviewed by a social worker and a psychologist. Then a lawyer will tell you your case will be closed if you are not caught again for three months, but if you are, there will be "serious consequences." You will probably smile inwardly at that for you know that the consequences might be a couple of hours of community service.[85]

A small homogeneous country, Portugal has a population of about 10 million with a hard core of "problem drug users" numbering about 100,000, or 1%. This was below the drug use level of most other countries, but, there were highly publicized drug slums developing where junkies scrounged for a life as awful as the fabled "les Misérables". This was not a welcome sight and so the administration decided to do something about it. They chose decriminalization on the recommendations of a panel of experts on the premise these drug users are sick not criminal. When addicts are caught and sent in for counseling they are invited to begin treatment paid for by the State. There are not a lot of these. In Lisbon, for example, only about 4 or 5 people per day with drugs in possession are sent in to the warning commission and 75% of those are marijuana only users.[86]

Today, Portugal is happy with this approach. They feel it is more humane and gets more addicts into treatment. They have not seen a substantial increase in drug use, and teen use appears to have dropped a little. They had considered legalization, but decided not to go that far.[87]

ARGUMENTS FOR LEGALIZATION

The Civil Liberties Argument

Television's John Stossel argues that "adults should be free to ingest whatever they want, knowing they are responsible for their actions." The civil liberties argument is also advanced by Cussen and Block, who wrote:

> The legalization of drugs would prevent our civil liberties from being threatened any further, it would reduce crime rates, reverse the potency effect, improve the quality of life in the inner cities, prevent the spread of disease, save the taxpayer money, and generally benefit both individuals

and the community as a whole. ...Legalizing drugs would eliminate many inconsistencies, guarantee freedoms, and increase the effectiveness of the government's anti-drug beliefs....[88]

There is a strong and well-reasoned philosophical tradition that supports this view. It is consistent with our founding constitutional principles. I have a right to swing my fist as I like, so long as it does not go farther than the end of your nose. As a people, we tend to favor this tradition because of its dynamism and promotion of wisdom through trial and error. In a long ago famous dictum by the Supreme Court Justice Oliver Wendell Holmes, he spoke of the truth that emerges from the marketplace of ideas. Freedom to speak and do as we please ought to be our default position as long as it does not deprive others of their same rights. Legalization of drug use would likely give us far more experience and information, which could help us to become wiser about drugs, an experience of which we deprive society by pushing their use underground. Whether that advantage is outweighed by foreseeable harm in terms of increased use by teens and preteens and in numbers of addicts remains debatable.

Legalization would reduce crime

During the Carter administration of the late 1970's, Surgeon General Jocelyn Elders announced her view that legalization would greatly reduce crime rates and should be studied. Later, a prominent professor, Steven Duke, argued that the *only* avenue then available toward the reduction of crime was some form of legalization.[89] Even law enforcement officers, when polled at a conference in 1995, believed our laws against drug use were "doing a lot of harm in contributing to murders, homicides, violence, corruption, the deterioration of inner cities and youth, and ...(had) disastrous racial consequences."[90] In a 2004 survey of police chiefs, 67% believed that law enforcement had *not been* successful in reducing (not even just "reducing") the drug problem in their communities, and 84% believed major changes are called for in drug policy.[91] In 2010, former Seattle Police Chief and author Norm Stamper argued for legalization of marijuana as a way of reducing crime and freeing up the police to "concentrate on crimes that inflict the deepest fear, pain and loss: burglaries, robberies, sexual assaults, domestic violence, stalking, child abuse, workplace and school shootings, drunk driving". He listed the consequences of the laws against marijuana:

> ...full employment for greedy people; criminal records attached to the lives of tens of millions of Americans; fractured families; inflated risks for cops; widespread discrimination against young, poor and black and brown people; exploitation and despoliation of thousands of acres of national park lands; open-air drug markets and deflated property values; public corruption; a brutal and bloody war raging in Mexico, now spilling over into the U.S., abridgement of our civil liberties, and the squandering of tens of billions of taxpayer dollars.[92]

Legalizing drug use would allow us to correctly treat it as a health issue

As early as the 1960s, there were many who argued that drug abuse and addiction are health problems than criminal behavior. Even then the view was expressed that addiction is not caused by drugs, but is an underlying problem that simply attaches itself to drug use as its path to relief from an unendurable life—or at least a life the young person believes is unendurable. This understanding has been supported by scientific research over the decades since then showing that there are biological and psychological factors which explain why some who take up drugs will become addicted, while the majority do not.[93] For example, kids with ADHD (Attention Deficit Hyperactivity Disorder) take up drugs at a higher rate than those without it. For some people, once the brain experiences the drug's effect it becomes unusually difficult to resist taking it again and addiction may follow. Genetics are believed to often play a role in addiction. We are inhumanely incarcerating people for suffering a mental aberration, and for a condition usually resulting from developmental problems that can be traced to infancy.[94]

Prohibition of drug use is ineffective and unjust.

Two important contributors to the literature, law professor Douglas Husak,[95]and Judge James Gray, (Ret'd)[96] have both made detailed arguments criticizing the injustice and ineffectiveness of our laws against drugs. Both argue for allowing adults freely to buy legally manufactured narcotics. By legalizing possession and use, they point out, the black market will be destroyed and end the access to drugs by minors. Judge Gray's book, which includes letters and comments from many other judges and justices, was endorsed by former Treasury Secretary, Secretary of State, and Senior Fellow at the Hoover Institute George P. Schultz, Nobel Prize economist Milton Friedman., the popular and trusted T.V. commentator, the late Walter Cronkite, and New Mexico governor, Gary Johnson.

Globally prominent leaders have also harshly criticized the use of criminal law in the effort to curtail drug use. The 2011 *Report of the Global Commission on Drug Use* said:

> ...drug policies were initially developed and implemented in the hope of achieving outcomes in terms of a reduction in harms to individuals and society – less crime, better health, and more economic and social development."

But, the commission concluded, the

> ... "war on drugs has failed, with devastating consequences for individuals and societies around the world," and that

"fundamental reforms in national and global drug control policies are urgently needed.[97]

Among the recommendations made by the Commission are that governments should be encouraged to experiment "with models of legal regulation of drugs (with cannabis, for example) that are designed to undermine the power of organized crime and safeguard the health and security of their citizens."[98]

Drug use prohibition has a disparate impact on minorities

The war on drugs, whether by design as some claim, or by unintended effect, has resulted in a counterproductive mass incarceration of African Americans.[99] The stigma effect of a criminal record, which affects a white person's ability to find employment, is magnified for blacks. Moreover, by a wide margin, the seeming disparate impact of drug prohibition on the black community fosters animosity toward the justice system. This may have a variety of consequences, including making it difficult for blacks to serve impartially as jurors in some cases. A Pew Research Center survey found that 70% of blacks believe they are less fairly treated by police than whites, and 68% do not trust the courts to deliver fair results.[100]

The perception of bias in the black community is an unfortunate reality, though it may be erroneous. Ian Tuttle offers some insights.[101]The reasons why more blacks are arrested is a complex one. There has been a clear disproportionate sentencing of those, mostly blacks, convicted of crack cocaine, compared to powder cocaine. However published data do not support the conclusion that the war on drugs disproportionately targets blacks as some have claimed. In 1980, *state* prisoners were 46.6% black and black federal prisoners made up 34.4% of the population. By 1990, 48.9% of state prisoners and 31.4% of federal prisoners were black. In a 2006 study the black percentage of state prisoners was found to be 37.5% of the 1,274,600-prisoner population, but if drug convictions were removed the percentage of black prisoners dropped to only 37%. That mere half percentage point drop suggests most black prisoners were there on non-drug convictions. The researchers concluded that throughout these time periods the reasons for black incarceration had much more to do with violent crimes in the black community than simple drug crime.[102]

However, the ACLU reported that blacks are 3.7 times more likely to be arrested on marijuana charges than whites despite similar usage rates. This data point, they argue, demonstrates racial profiling. But, the ACLU admits it did not control for important other factors such as "individual characteristics of each arrest, such as amount of marijuana possessed and criminal history record of the individual arrested." If more drug dealing occurs in the black communities than in the white, and the police are keener on action against dealing, then the failure to control for those characteristics weakens the ACLU analysis.[103] However, I would argue that whether the perceived racial disparity in the drug war is an illusion or real, it is heartfelt among millions of our African American neighbors and friends and it provides an additional reason to dispense with the war on drugs.

ARGUMENTS AGAINST LEGALIZATION

We need controls to protect against use by adolescents

Associate Professor of Philosophy at Arizona State University Peter de Marneffe argues that there would be insufficient controls under legalization to prevent leakage into the hands of minors.[104] Teenagers can be quite resourceful in arranging for access to alcohol. Why would they be less so if drugs were sold in the same way?

Former Congressman Patrick Kennedy, in a letter to Attorney General Eric Holder, strenuously argued that Holder should take steps to enforce the Controlled Substances Act as against the states of Washington and Colorado, whose citizens had recently voted for adoption of laws legalizing the purchase and sale of marijuana. He said:

> Marijuana remains a leading reason kids are in treatment today, and is a leading cause of car crashes among impaired individuals – surpassing alcohol in many states. Its abuse is directly linked to mental illness and IQ deterioration. The negative impacts of legalization of marijuana are substantial.... We advocate for an education-oriented strategy to prevent marijuana use, with focus on early intervention and treatment of addiction as a health issue. We also need to make sure those in recovery are not stigmatized for their addiction. State laws legalizing marijuana would severely hamper our ability to act in the interest of public health. We urge you to swiftly and publicly declare these state laws illegal.[105]

The letter shows a robust opposition by drug court professionals and the medical profession (see the co-authors in the footnote) to legalization, because of the potential for great harm to children. Yet the quoted passage calls for prevention of drug use through education and treatment and notes the need to avoid the stigma that attaches to drug users branded as criminals. How Mr. Kennedy and friends think these needs can be fulfilled in a prohibition regime is left unexplained. His claim that marijuana "abuse is directly linked to mental illness and IQ deterioration," is not settled scientifically and is disputed by many. The point that stigma is caused by criminal punishment is, of course, one of the arguments of those who favor legalization. We should note also that it is debatable whether pot is a leading cause of impaired driving. Studies have contradicted this claim. It is true, however, that the risk of auto accidents rises dramatically when the driver has consumed both alcohol and marijuana.

Prohibition discourages drug use.

Several proponents of drug use prohibition who were directly involved in initiating the war on drugs recently argued that it has been effective. Their argument is based on the improvement in "past month" usage data following adoption of the national Substance Control Act. In a letter to the Wall Street Journal,[106] they said:

> The rate of past-month use of illicit drugs by Americans age 12 and older declined 38% from its peak of 14.1% in 1979 to 8.7% in 2011. ... In 2011, 51.8% of Americans used alcohol, 26.5% used tobacco and only 8.7% used any of the illegal drugs in the past month (7% used marijuana). The much lower rates of use of illegal drugs are not the result of a difference in their effect on brain biology. They are the result of their being illegal.

Correlation is not the same as causation. We can accept the statement that the lower rate of use of the hard drugs is not the result of a different effect on brain biology, without jumping from there to the conclusion drawn by these letter writers. All these drugs were illegal in the States before the Substance Abuse Act of 1970, yet many in the baby boomer generation were using them in defiance of the law. No doubt, the likelihood that the new war on drugs laws had some impact. Even some of the "flower children" who thought they derived inspiration from their LSD hallucinations and the "laid back" pleasures of marijuana, must have come to their senses in part because of the increased risk of jail time. As noted elsewhere, Kleiman et.al, along with others, supports the view that the threat of punishment is for many an effective deterrent. [107] However, there may well have been other changes in the culture as the baby boomers matured and knowledge of the risks spread more widely. In any event the drop of 5.4% difference in the percentage of past month users is less impressive when we consider the fact that new designer drugs started coming in from China, which were not picked up in the statistics.

All we need is more treatment and prevention

President Obama's Office of Narcotic Drug Control Policy (ONDCP) continues to favor enforcement of existing law. In a February 14, 2013, a blog post titled "Toward a Smarter Drug Policy", co-authored by R. Gil Kerlikowske, Director, ONDCP and Benjamin Todd Jealous, President and CEO, NAACP, which called for a "fundamental shift," in the discussion, the disproportionate harshness of current policy on the black community was mentioned and uneasiness with the criminal punishment system was revealed. But what the President would do about it is described in this passage:

> Armed with the indisputable fact that preventing and treating addiction is an effective strategy for reducing substance abuse and crime, the Obama Administration and the NAACP are committed to pursuing evidence-based policies that strengthen families and communities across America.[108]

This statement describes existing policies. The administration, it seems, was little motivated to make serious reform efforts and the policy of trying to prevent and treat addiction solely with education and more rehab continues.

Drug use is immoral and de-stigmatizing drug use will encourage more of it, especially among the young.

William J. Bennett, a CNN Contributor who has served both as a White House Drug Czar and Secretary of Education, on June 30, 2011, again reiterated his now familiar case against "legalization schemes," as he refers to legalization and decriminalization. Among his arguments he claims:

> Normalizing, de-stigmatizing, and legalizing illegal drugs lowers their price and increases their use as has been shown by a recent RAND study on California. RAND estimated legalization of marijuana there would cut the price by as

much as 80% and increase use from as little as 50% to as much as 100%.

In a book co-authored by Bennett in 1995, he argued that drug use is morally wrong, quoting the eminent criminologist, the late James Q. Wilson, to that effect.[109]

Bennett deserves respect as a public servant and as a public intellectual. However, he, like Wilson, is heavily invested in the morality issue. As I discuss elsewhere, morality alone is not a proper basis for prohibitive law. Everyone has the right to his or her own moral convictions and emotions. Our "government of laws and not of men" should not impose the moral views of those holding policy making powers upon all the rest. Moreover, ample evidence is now available to refute the notion that a drug tolerant reform would increase drug use.

The System Proposed Satisfies Both Positions.

This debate has been going on for a long time and divides the people of the U.S. about in half. The people have acquiesced in the costs and lack of results of prohibition, I contend, only because we have assumed outlawing drugs for everyone as the only way to control them. This, I show, is a mistaken assumption. It is possible to be tough and smart at the same time.

Still, there is reason to disagree with those who would decriminalize the use of street drugs, or allow adults to buy legal drugs as suggested by Judge Gray, in retail stores, with prohibition of sales to minors as the only control mechanism.[110] Something more than a ban on sales to minors is clearly needed. Today, minors obtain beer, wine and liquor almost at will, either with fake IDs or with the help of adults willing to buy for them. Nor can I embrace ideas suggested by others such as allowing drugs to be bought with a doctor's prescription, or in legally limited amounts at the pharmacy. Though these approaches would dent the illegal trade, they would not kill it. And selling in pharmacies with or without a doctor's prescription would likely make drugs too expensive to compete with the illegal trade. The minors would still have access to illegal drugs. Moreover, without assurance against access by minors, these ideas won't likely be *politically* feasible.

The System is based upon the destruction of the illegal market with the market forces of a legal one. We see how that works in Chapter 5. Accompanied by counseling and additional control measures to prevent sharing with minors, it should find support on both sides of the political divide. While killing the illegal drug trade, it would bring addicts out of the shadows and into the light of scientific knowledge and the friendly influence of professional counselors, who work like coaches. The monitoring element enables the counselors to identify potential client problems of abuse and to take corrective steps. Monitoring, together with the remote purchase feature, makes it impracticable for an adult user to purchase and sell to others. The only way minors could obtain drugs would be from System clients. Limiting the amounts clients may purchase at any one time would discourage failure to protect against access by others, including minors.

The need of drug users for more and better information

A valuable feature of the System proposed, and one easily overlooked by skeptics, is the educational component. An adult drug user would not be allowed to go on using drugs without up-to-date information. They would be required to sit down and listen to what they need to know of the ever-advancing discoveries of science.

It is especially important to emphasize to them the harm of drugs to minors. As the above cited paper of NIDA's Volkow shows, that is the age of greatest vulnerability to addiction. I repeat for emphasis, nine in ten adult addicts got their start between the ages of 12 through 17. Young people, even well into their twenties are more vulnerable than the more mature, because of the way the brain develops. Its propensity for adventurism is in place by puberty, while the pre-frontal cortex where sound judgment and self-control reside, does not arrive until a dozen or more years later. Adult users need to be taught these facts and to understand that if they share drugs with youngsters or encourage drug use by them, they are subjecting them to a heightened risk of addiction, and themselves to being kicked out of the program. Only a minority of adolescent drug users will become addicted, but adults who encourage minors to use, even when it's only marijuana, are playing Russian roulette with those young lives: they do not know which are vulnerable to addiction.

Chapter 5:

Call in the Economists

In my opinion, economists and sociologists are the people to whom we ought to turn more than we do for instruction in the grounds and foundations of all rational decisions.

Justice Oliver Wendell Holmes

Economists such as Edmund Phelps, who argues persuasively for the value of dynamism to every aspect of economic performance; Milton Friedman who explained how the vast power of a free market stems from human nature; and Joseph Schumpeter who emphasized the "gales of creative destruction" sweeping over the world for the benefit of mankind, all teach us that if we want to kill the illegal drug trade, we have the means at hand to do so. These luminaries and their many colleagues both contemporary and historic put beyond question the central theme of this book, that legal, free market forces can defeat the illegal trade in a way that the war on drugs only could hope for—and take drugs out of the reach of the young.

We do not need to study the academics, though, to understand how a legitimate market in chemically pure drugs manufactured by licensed and regulated pharmaceutical companies would destroy the black market in drugs. When we look back and round about us, we see many demonstrations of how economic forces work to destroy markets. If I mention that our use of computers and word processors has destroyed the market for typewriters, some readers will wonder: *what's a typewriter?* Older readers may remember loading film into a camera--Kodak was a household name--but probably can't remember the last time they paid to have it "developed." Not long ago we all wrote letters on stationery, stuffed them in envelopes, pasted on postage stamps, and took them to a mailbox. Now we mostly touch "send" to deliver letters electronically, and expect a reply by the same means. These examples of dynamism reveal a constant of the free market. Cars replaced the horse drawn buggies, and now we expect soon to ride in self-driving cars. Industry caters to human nature: the human preference for what is better, quicker or cheaper. Creative destruction occurs to satisfy those preferences. Amazon has entered our lives "bigtime." Today we are inured to the wireless world for communication, learning and entertainment. The chronicler of high tech, Michael Malone pities the movie industry. As he puts it: "Getting the under-25 audience to abstain from social media for two hours and sit in a dark auditorium is increasingly difficult." Life patterns change as new opportunities arise.

How better, quicker, cheaper would destroy the illegal drug trade.

The profits of the drug traffickers and dealers come in the main from hard-core adult users--the regular and frequent users who use drugs daily, year in and year out. Unlike low budget teenagers, these people spend thousands per year on their habits. If that business were lost to the traffickers, their numbers would plummet and the small-scale dealers and user-dealers would go the way of buggy whip and photo film makers.

So, what does the System offer that is better, quicker, and cheaper to the adult drug users? Clients of the System would purchase drugs at well below street prices, or receive them free if necessary to remove the motive to commit crime to afford them. Legal drugs are far *cheaper* than illegal drugs. The drugs would be manufactured by licensed pharmaceutical companies in their modern high-tech labs. Legal drugs are *better*, because chemically pure—they are free of additives and stretchers that often pose dangers to health—users know exactly what they are getting with the potency controlled. This reduces the risk of overdose. New and safer legal products could be designed also to improve health and safety. Acquiring drugs is *quicker* and easier here. There are no more delays due to getting money to pay high street prices, or trekking to a distant dealer, or seeking other sources when one's dealer has been arrested or is in hiding— or inventories have temporarily dried up in the area because of DEA interdictions. The client enjoys reliable delivery at pre-determined intervals – no waiting and no uncertainty about supply.

And then the icing on the cake. Even more attractive to drug users than all the rest is that clients in good standing need never again fear arrest and punishment for possessing or using drugs— as long as their drugs were System dispensed.

Skeptics question whether the illegal trade can really be killed. Experience has already begun to prove the theory valid. When medical marijuana was introduced in Colorado, dealers in counties allowing it, moved on to other counties where it was scarce. The price of marijuana had dropped so much that it was no longer profitable for the peddlers to operate there.[111] The situation changed only now the state has legalized marijuana for recreation too. Taxation of recreational marijuana, raises the price so high the retailers cannot compete and the illicit market flourishes.[112]

Expect early resistance and gradual acceptance.

We should not expect immediate acceptance by all users. While we humans reliably embrace the better, the quicker and the cheaper, there is another feature of human nature: reluctance to change. We likely evolved this trait as we learned repeatedly over eons of time to distrust things that are not tried and true. In the roll-out of the proposed system, we should expect resistance from drug users unwilling to have their behavior overseen by others–who dislike the idea of being monitored. Some will resist being required to use only moderately and responsibly. Also, those who deal drugs as well as use, will likely be slow to give up on their business, hoping they can continue to make a go of it.

Over time, however, the roll out might look something like the following. Suppose you have a program serving a population of one million residents. Government data tell us that 7% or 70,000 of those residents are users of the various illegal drugs, mostly marijuana. The System begins slowly, but accelerates over time. Let's suppose the program has been well advertised and in the first year of operation 20% of the area's drug users sign up, taking 14,000 users out of the local drug market. The smallest of small-scale dealers give up the business or move to another locale. By the end of the following year another 20% have signed up and so now 28,000 have withdrawn their business from the illegal drug market. Dealers begin to leave–illegal drugs are harder to find and their availability less reliable. This makes joining the program even more attractive to the holdouts. With the next 20% entering the program, the acceleration of the moving out of the dealers has begun and holdout users struggle to find black market sources. The early holdouts are now giving in and taking the easier and cheaper way to have their drugs. The presence of drug dealers in the area is now so reduced that the police find it much easier, especially when aided by citizen vigilance, to roll up the remaining dealers. The lure of better, quicker, cheaper drugs has worked its powerful logic and overcome the objections to the control mechanisms of monitoring and counseling.

Does this illustration make it all sound too easy? Maybe so, and maybe the program will take much longer to mature and meet its goals. This is no reason to oppose it. In all business startups, there are snags and obstacles along the way. But the principles underlying this imagined scenario are well proven in legal markets and sufficiently so in illegal ones as well. We should not doubt the power of market forces, taught us in the lessons of history.

And notice, this is a scalable system. It can be started with experimental models in any small region, county or community where it is welcomed. There it will show how effective it can be, as the drug dealers move away looking for greener pastures. Other states will be encouraged to try their own programs, just as so many have on witnessing Seattle's LEAD program success. Over time we should expect the System to spread across the country.

Rational and Irrational Use of Drugs

Economic analysis is not limited to money matters in its ability to enlighten a discourse. It also provides a disciplined method for examining most all social issues. As a result, many economists have weighed in and have added useful insights. An interesting analysis by one such (Jeffrey Miron) in his book, *Drug War Crimes*, discusses the rational consumption I mentioned in Chapter One and invites us to consider that reduced drug consumption is not necessarily desirable. Rational drug consumption, Miron points out, may be a net good in society, without which society is the poorer. He sums up his discussion this way:

> The normative analysis of drug prohibition produces three key conclusions: First, virtually all the effects of prohibition are undesirable, with the *possible* exception of reduced consumption. Second, reduced drug consumption is not *necessarily* desirable; any reduction in *rational* drug consumption is a cost, not a benefit, of policies that reduce drug consumption. Third, even if reduced drug consumption is an appropriate goal for policy, prohibition is almost certainly the wrong approach.[113] (Emphasis added)

Rational consumption of drugs is the use which satisfies a need or a desire of an individual and is done without negative consequences that outweigh that benefit. One with anxiety disorder, for example, can obtain relief from a moderate dose of heroin. Some and probably most of the people who use heroin can do so without bad health effects. They have learned to use it moderately—rationally.

Most adult users of marijuana enjoy its calming or soothing quality without harmful effect, many more the pain relief or calming effects of both marijuana and the opiates. Today, research shows reduced heroin use in states allowing medical marijuana, and there is evidence that marijuana might be useful in treating opioid addiction. It is known to stave off opioid withdrawal. Others may experience better moods and productivity with cocaine, used in moderation, without harm to them or others.

If we want as gainful a society as we can achieve, then why would we not tolerate rational and responsible use of drugs? Many believe that all drug use is addicting, but today the science shows this is demonstrably false. Hart states that at least seventy five percent of users do not become addicted.[114] The paper of NIDA Director Volkow and colleagues, mentioned above, indicates that addiction occurs through a combination of prolonged use plus vulnerability affecting only about 10% of users.[115]

Economic perspective on the extent of drug use and addiction

There are, to be sure, many negative consequences of drug consumption by some. These include neglect of a child by a parent or guardian, whose judgment is impaired by drugs, abuse of others while on drugs, sexual predation of victims made more vulnerable by drugs, the drain on society's resources which may include loss of an abuser's productivity and the income taxes he might otherwise pay, and costs of medical care in treating both addiction and the increasing overdose cases. These behaviors certainly justify controls designed to curtail them. In the new System, no one gets a "get of jail free" card if drugs are used abusively or illegally. Moreover, in this System, anyone doing business with illicit dealers would be guilty of aiding and abetting a crime punishable by law. However, in thinking about how these effects can be reduced, as well as how to evaluate the System, we need to keep the issues in accurate perspective.

The SAMHSA survey[116] data indicate that about 27.0 million people aged 12 or older in 2014 were current illicit drug users. The number increases a little each year as the population also increases. In 2014, about 10 percent of the population aged 12 or older or 1 in 10 were current users and this was a slightly higher percentage than in 2013. So more than just population may account for the increase. The survey also shows the clear majority of users are marijuana only users. They number over 22 million of the 27 million.

In 2014 there were more than 2.3 million adolescents in the 12 to 17 age group currently using. This number approaches 10% of that age group.   And, recall the Volkow report indicates 1 in 10 current users are vulnerable to addiction. The age of minority extends to 21. In the age group 18 through 20 we have another 2.8 million or so current users. So, we can see that over 5 million of our 27 million current users are under age. Since they are the cohort most vulnerable to addiction, we can make huge inroads on the addiction problem by killing off the drug trade.

And, by introducing the counseling component, we will have taken giant step toward achieving responsible use among the adult users. Again, for emphasis, it is the under-age-21 people who grow into the huge pool of adult addicts, most of whom range in age up to early and mid-30s, and make the market depended upon by the traffickers. Interest in drug use drops off precipitously after age 21. Once a young person reaches adulthood, there are many more incentives such as education, employment, marriage and family and recreational opportunities to compete with drug use.

Nothing I say here is intended to suggest drug abuse and addiction do not pose serious problems in the U.S. Even though the number is small in relation to the population, drug abuse and addiction do contribute to the national costs of health care and criminal justice. Users do sometimes act in ways that are criminal, or disturbing or unsafe to themselves or others. The point of focus here, though, is that, despite the wide availability of drugs, we have not seen regular drug use turn into a societal norm, or a threat of broad cultural degeneration. We need to keep this perspective: drug use is not so prevalent, nor likely to become so widespread, in the new System, that we should continue to acquiesce in the greater harms and costly failures of our prohibition policies.

Several studies have shown that the problem of impaired driving is less frequently associated with marijuana use than with alcohol use.[117] And while it is a fair argument that we do not need in general circulation another substance that contributes to highway accidents, there is reason to expect that where marijuana is allowed, it is, for many, a substitute for alcohol. To that extent it does not add to the problem of intoxicated driving, but reduces it by replacing alcohol with a less troublesome drug. In those states that choose to include marijuana in the System, there is no reason to fear increased irresponsible use, and every reason to expect more responsible use: that is, a lowered rate of marijuana DUI. Why? Because, in time, teenage access to it will be lower and irresponsible drug use by adults will be discouraged by the risk of ouster from the System's program.

Assessing the costs of our pursuit of prohibition.

Costs in Human Capital

By human capital we mean the talents, the physical strengths, the knowledge and acquired skills, the ingenuity and the abilities of the people who make up our economy, our communities, and our culture.

My interest in the problems of our war on drugs was in part aroused many years ago by a news article about a young California school administrator whom I will fictionally call Martin Vargas. The account described him as highly regarded by teachers and students in his school district. But, he had been arrested for dealing drugs. He had been on a successful career track in which he would predictably have continued as a helpful role model for and educator to thousands of children. But, for some reasons he fell to the temptation to sell a drug. Martin was confronted by the police at his school in the presence of fellow teachers, administrators and students, handcuffed, put into a squad car, and taken to be booked into jail. It is tempting to speculate about why such a man would jeopardize his career in such a way. Maybe he had a bit of a drug problem and needed to deal a little to afford it. Maybe he was suffering financial difficulties and dealing became an easy solution. These are not excuses for law breaking, but is it not a clear waste to destroy such careers? In a use tolerant system, such a temptation as lured Martin would not exist.

There are many who take the hard line that this guy deserved what he got. But, here's the question. Given the moral ambiguity that surrounds drugs, should we treat such conduct the same as other law breaking? Alcohol is a much more addicting and harmful drug than marijuana, yet it is legally sold to adults and many, including high schoolers, party with booze on weekends, along with cigarettes. Cigarettes are also addicting and kill many thousands more than drugs. Marijuana is legal in eight states and D.C. Martin's judgment may have been clouded, but, it is difficult in my judgment to justify the crushing treatment he suffered before he even got to court. The day I read about him was the day I began to ask how we justify a drug control system that is so ineffective in reducing drug use and curtailing the trafficking, while making criminals of users and small-scale sellers in the first place.

It is not sympathy for Martin that makes this story relevant, but the losses sustained by all of us. Taxpayers spent a good deal of money providing him the education that made him a school district asset. Martin himself invested a good deal of his life and energy into developing the knowledge, experience and skills to become a productive educator. This is one form of human capital loss. As with the many stories of police officers corrupted by drugs, it occurs when human nature is subjected to the temptations of the drug market—a business opportunity that could not exist without our prohibition regime.

Another illustration which, though fictional, is realistic, comes to us in the series made for TV, "Breaking Bad."   Here we meet Walter White, an excellent chemistry teacher, whose doctor had diagnosed a tumor certain to kill him in a year or so. His death could mean destitution for a wife, who is pregnant, and a severely disabled son, both of whom he loved very much. When he learns that large sums of money can be quickly made in the production of methamphetamine, the decision practically makes itself: he will use his chemistry knowledge to make the best meth on the market. He will be a good producer, making a chemically pure product. He will be able to leave his wife and children a better life than they could hope for. We can all agree that his sad circumstances do not justify his chosen criminal conduct. In our society, we do not get to choose which laws we will obey. Yet there is another compelling question. Wouldn't we be better off without laws against adult drug use that make such activities profitable?   In a system that allowed adult users to buy and use drugs legally, the prices would be so low, and the underground market so unprofitable, the Walter Whites of the world could not find it profitable to make and sell illegal drugs. Chances are their talents would be turned to productive endeavors.

Loss of human capital occurs also when we put people in jail. Adam Brown (his real name) was addicted to crack cocaine. He had been convicted and jailed multiple times on drug charges. After he died, his parents and his widow were interviewed on television. According to them he had overcome his addiction to crack, on his own volition, motivated by his desire to become a Navy Seal. He accomplished that goal. This would be a remarkable story even if it had ended there, but there is more. To be accepted as a Seal requires great focus, dedication and extraordinary effort, none of which are usually associated with the drug addict. Still he achieved that, and then, after losing the use of his right arm, he trained himself to shoot left handed–so well in fact he was able again to qualify for active duty as a Navy Seal. He served with such dedication his fellow Seals were in awe of him. He died a highly decorated soldier in combat in the Kumar Province, Afghanistan in 2010, gunned down as he moved forward into enemy fire to protect his team. His achievements and heroism are inspiring. They are also testaments to the potential and worth of even those who once seemed lost to drugs. Adam accomplished all that after multiple arrests and convictions for cocaine use. How much more success might he have achieved had he been free of the interruptions, setbacks and stigma of repeated criminal arrest, arraignment, conviction and sentencing to time in prison? We may stipulate that he had a choice and he chose to break the laws against drugs and therefore brought on his own punishment. How much sooner might he have matured and developed positive goals without the wasted time and disruptions inflicted in the criminal justice system? Under the new System, he would have been coached toward responsible drug use, and aided by his counselor to envision his potentials without drugs much sooner. And during that time, he would have been free to develop his education along with his maturity.

Standing alone the two cases of Martin and Adam might seem like aberrations or outliers. Martin is not the kind of guy who usually gets caught up in drug dealing. Adam Brown was a unique individual with unusual strengths. But as the experts show, there are many productive and valuable individuals who take up drugs and use them without destructive consequences. Those charged and treated as criminals are taken out of their productive work, or education, stigmatized, and diminished in their potentials. We should abhor the waste of human time, spirit, reputation, productivity and social stability that results from the criminal punishment of people with the potential for productive lives. We know that jailing people for nothing more than using a drug or selling some to help make ends meet is of no net benefit to society. The waste of human talent directly caused by the criminal punishment of people like Adam and Martin, even though its effect may only be temporary, represents a cost to society of incalculable proportions—and no justification in drug use reduction.

In another true story, U.S. Army veteran Scott C., who had served in Afghanistan, died early on the summery southern Oregon evening of June 2012. He was 44 years of age and enrolled at Rogue Community College. According to the report of his mother he was working toward a nursing degree. She also said that he had been suffering from post-traumatic stress disorder, as many returning veterans do, but had been managing it. Scott was a gentle person, his step-daughter told me, not given to violence.

What happened to Scott, happens in all too many drug arrests. Scott's mother had called 911 earlier that evening because Scott was acting strangely. She said he had not slept for five days and that he was coming off a methamphetamine high. The 911 operator alerted the police and emergency medical services. Two police officers confronted Scott and spent 20 or 30 minutes trying to persuade him to accept handcuffs and come with them to the hospital. He would seem calm for a time and then become agitated and move from room to room. When the officers tried to handcuff him he physically resisted. After a warning, they used the taser. He fell to the floor and they cuffed him. Then his breathing became shallow. Now afraid for his life, the officers rushed him to the hospital, but he was dead on arrival. The autopsy concluded the cause of death was "complications of methamphetamine intoxication." There were complications all right, especially when the police arrived.

Some will say it was Scott's fault and I do not suggest criticism of the police. They acted in accordance with their training and protocols. Their focus was on the enforcement part of law enforcement. Sparse information makes it difficult to assign fault in such cases. Certainly, Scott bore responsibility, but we should not say he killed himself–and certainly not that he deserved to die for his behavior. Scott had taken a stimulate, much like others commonly used in the military to promote alertness and focus. He may have assumed his training and experience made it safe for him to use. His was a mistake in judgment, not a profound moral lapse.

Meth addicts can and often do mature out of their drug use and end addiction both with and without treatment. Suppose the first responders had been trained medics instead of police. There would not have been the implied threat of arrest and being booked into jail. As he was not offering violence toward anyone a taser would not have been used. The System I propose offers a common-sense alternative approach that would likely have both served our interest keeping the peace, and avoiding injury to one needing medical help. And, Scott C. might well be alive and working as a nurse today. He might have used his experience with methamphetamine to help others with a similar problem.

Still as many times as such deaths have occurred since drug prohibition, they are not the greatest squandering of human capital it causes. That distinction goes to what the U.S. Attorney General has called the "warehousing" of able-bodied men and women who present no threat of violent crime to society.

Possession of illicit drugs, except for marijuana in the few that allow it, is a crime in all 50 states and, with no exception, under federal law; arrestees go into the justice system in large numbers and repeaters get jail time. How well does this serve our purposes, really? Is a young adult who has developed an addiction, but is keeping his use to a level that permits him to function reasonably well on his job or in high school or college the kind of person we want to see sitting in a jail for days, weeks or months, often just long enough so that he loses the job or the ability to complete his schooling on schedule?

Shortly before writing these sentences, I read of a local writing teacher honored for her essays and poetry. I happen to know that many years ago as a young student in a New England state, she used and dealt cocaine for a time while working as a server in an upscale restaurant where customers often indulged. How fortunate we are that, unlike many, a criminal record did not ruin her life. In another example, the distinguished writer/journalist Maia Szalavitz tells in her 2016 book, *Unbroken Brain*, of her struggle in her early years with heroin, dealing cocaine to pay for it, and shooting up as many as 40 times per day. She came to her senses after being arrested, but a forward-thinking judge gave her another chance. She took it and succeeded in quitting largely on her own. How does it serve society to jail and stigmatize such people? Yet we do it and lose the human capital of thousands across the country each year–an incalculable waste of productive potential avoidable an intelligent system.

The Financial Costs

Calculating the money cost of our present approach to drugs in America is a daunting task. The cost in dollars and cents includes many things which are hard to measure. What does it cost us in dollars when a fine teacher is taken out of the classroom because he succumbed to the temptation to sell some marijuana to supplement his income? What are the dollar cost ramifications, impacting two or more generations, when a child's mom goes to jail and that child has difficulties dealing emotionally with the calamity? What is the lost value occasioned when a Dad is snatched from his family because he was unable or unwilling to give up his drug, though he could hold down a job and support them? What about the damage to employment prospects of those with arrest records and the shrinkage of our work force when they leave it in frustration? Today we are seeing increasing numbers of older convicts returning to prison, bringing medical conditions not common among young convicts. How do we compute the health care costs associated with them? Changing standards in law enforcement practices make policing more expensive and difficult to quantify, just as increased costs for facilities and personnel in the court system spiral upward. We could go on and on imagining the ways our pursuit of prohibition is costing more dollars each year, but the point is sufficiently clear. Our use of criminal punishment to control drugs has many and varied costs difficult to put a number on, though we know it's a big one. During his life, Nobel economist Gary Becker posted blogs with the highly esteemed federal judge, Judge Richard Posner. In 2005, Becker wrote that a study by him and colleagues indicated that number was about $100 Billion per year. And this was without counting "important intangible costs, such as the destructive effects on many inner-city neighborhoods, the use of the American military to fight drug lords and farmers in Colombia and other nations, or the corrupting influence of drugs on many governments."[118]Legalization of all the now illicit drugs would, he concludes, "be a far cheaper and more effective way to reduce drug use."

Yet, a larger proportion of U.S. residents are doing prison time for drug law violations than are behind bars for all offenses put together in any country to which we would like to be compared, according to Mark A.R. Kleiman, Editor of "Drug Policy Analysis". The state and national drug policies are enormously costly in money, time and effort. We spend $40 billion per year at the federal level—much more at the state level–just on prevention and treatment, law enforcement, interdiction and international programs, which aim to change the ways of the opium, pot and coke farmers. Are we getting our money's worth? For sure, we have incarcerated many, including the Adam Browns of the world, but as we have seen that is not the kind of success we really hoped for.

Over two million individuals are presently incarcerated in federal and state jails and prisons. There are twice as many on probation or parole. The U.S. incarcerates a quarter of all the world's prison inmates. According to the Justice Policy Institute in 2009, the United States incarcerated roughly 10 times as many people as the U.K., Canada, Australia, Germany and Finland, combined, although it has only about 1/3 more people than the total of those nations. As noted earlier most were on drugs or alcohol when arrested and many of these inmates are there on drug charges alone. For the most part, we do not incarcerate first time use offenders, but Attorney General Eric Holder argues that far too many populate our jails and prisons for nothing more than repeated drug use.

The cost of incarceration varies by state but in California it is approximately $47,000 per year for each individual prisoner. The average across the country is lower at about $30,000. Drug Czar Gil Kerlikowski tells us that the high rates of incarceration have resulted in prison overcrowding and state governments facing the costs of a rapidly expanding penal system.

In addition to the billions spent on prison costs there are the salaries we pay the police who make the arrests. New York City arrests 50,000 each year. Most other cities in the U.S. rival New York's arrest rate on a per capita basis. We also pay the salaries of judges, both federal and state and their court staff clerks and officers. Then there are all the costs associated with maintaining the courtrooms necessary to handle the workload of drug related arrests, and the costs of maintaining huge staffs of probation and parole officers to monitor released convicts.

We also spend money outside the country. In one example, according to the Government Accountability Office (GAO), over the five years from 2006 through 2011, we sent $5.182 billion of federal taxpayer dollars to the Andean countries of Peru, Columbia, Bolivia, Ecuador and Venezuela for use in efforts for counter narcotics assistance, but with little in reported progress. Through the years the GAO has not been able to report any substantial curtailment of the coca paste production there.[119]

We all should be glad to pay these costs if they were keeping the drugs out of the hands of the teenagers and young adults where most drug use starts. But, the evidence points the other way. And what more effective use of funds might these expenditures be crowding out? Are we thinking through the problems of drugs in society, or just reacting emotionally and equating dollars spent with progress?

Property crimes, "acquisitive crimes," represent another major financial cost both to taxpayers who pay for law enforcement, and to the victims of those crimes. Drug use prohibition causes higher prices by forcing drug traffickers and dealers to evade law enforcement–a costly process, involving expensive smuggling, hush money bribes and the like. When the DEA and the police outsmart the traffickers, and interdict a large shipment of drugs, scarcity is increased and prices go higher. But, economists show drug demand is inelastic, meaning higher prices do not reduce drug consumption. Addicts feel they must fund the habit that enslaves them. Crime is the frequent result. And when prices rise higher so does crime. It is difficult to find a well-supported estimate of the number of drug users who commit crimes to pay for drugs. However, researchers in 1998 found that alcohol and drug problems were at work in influencing the behavior of 80% of prison inmates and most of them will return to a life of alcohol and drug abuse and crime, committing as many as 100 crimes per day to fund their habits.[120] Crime committed to buy drugs includes dealing and prostitution, thefts, burglaries, car jackings, purse snatching, shoplifting and armed robbery. It also includes identity theft and frauds and scams of various kinds. Drug users who turned to crime and succeeded in it once are likely to do it repeatedly. A study in England has estimated that law enforcement dealing with these drug related crimes comes at a cost equal to 1.6% of GDP (a measure of the annual economic output) and they are not as aggressive as we are in the U.S.

We are long overdue for a cost/benefit analysis and an overhaul of our thinking of whether these costs borne by society are justified by results in use reduction.

Indirect burdens on the national economy

The fiscal health of our states and cities is of critical importance to our national economy, job growth and rising standards of living. The states and cities bear the main burden (75%) of needed infrastructure facilities such as roads, bridges, sewage treatment, and water. Classroom costs (K-12) are borne 90% by state governments.[121] According to the Federal Reserve Bank, as of the third quarter of 2011, state and local governments were in debt by $2.99 trillion, nearly all of it long term, with interest payments adding to the burden. All together these governments outspend the federal government on goods and services, making up roughly 12% of our national GDP. [122]

Increasing taxes by many of these local governments has become difficult as their electorates, in some cases, see themselves as already over-taxed, and others are struggling with unfavorable employment and business conditions where more taxation might worsen those problems. Appreciating the importance of maintaining our schools, infrastructure, and medical aid for the poor, we should look at our pursuit of prohibition as a financial impairment of those state and local programs, impacting the very economic strength of the country.

Edward Prescott writing in the Quarterly Review of the Federal Reserve Bank of Minneapolis, showed that taxes on earnings and consumer spending, which include federal, state and local income taxes, Social Security and Medicare payroll taxes, excise taxes, and state and local sales taxes, put the U.S. average marginal effective tax rate at 40%.[123] At a time when policy makers in the nation's capital and the Congressional Budget Office warn of impending need for more taxation to cover the entitlement obligations of Medicare, social security and the like, something has to give. Drug use prohibition is a logical part of that something.

High quality jobs in large numbers.

The System I propose will eliminate jobs in the justice and prison systems, but it will create high quality jobs in large numbers. There are at any given time numbers of unemployed and under-employed teachers, nurses, clinical psychologists, probation officers, police officers, and others of various levels of learning and experience who, with minimal training would be well qualified to enter this new field of drug use counseling. In addition, new college graduates are always in generous supply. Large numbers of college graduates, with majors in English literature, sociology, psychology, anthropology, business administration and so on want employment, but find little demand in the conventional marketplace for the narrow area of their learning. It is estimated that we have 115,520 janitors in the United States with education at the level of bachelor's degrees and higher. Many young men and women find themselves after college in occupations they never dreamed of, but glad to be employed.

The counselor staff of System operators will come from all areas of learning and experience. Persons of college graduate age, typically 22, are generally open minded about a career and receptive to additional training that can equip them for such a high-quality job as drug use counseling promises to be. In time colleges and universities will offer semester courses designed to fit students for work in this field.

Many thousands of counselors would be needed across the country. In addition, many more employees would be needed to perform all the administrative, technical, warehousing and delivery functions. While the purpose of the System proposed is not to create jobs, this clearly will be a happy by-product of it.

Chapter 6:

How Biases Clog Minds and Obstruct Policy Dynamism

I think unconscious bias is one of the hardest things to get at.

Justice Ruth Bader Ginsburg

...all our knowledge grows only through the correcting of our mistakes."

Karl Popper

In Chapter 1 we exposed some of the myths messing up public awareness around the world. We know that drugs do not *cause* addiction; they do not *cause* unemployment; and they do not *cause* moral degeneration. Over 65% of regular users of illegal drugs are working in full or part- time jobs. Regular drug use, as opposed to abuse, does not induce moral degeneration characterized by crime, violence or other anti-social behaviors.[124]

As NIDA director Volkow and her colleagues show, the cause of addiction lies in the personality development of certain individuals, resulting from genetic and environmental factors. The lack of employment results from irresponsible behaviors, crime convictions, underdeveloped coping skills, and failure to acquire necessary education or training. Certainly, irresponsible drug use can contribute to these, but we cannot say the properties of the drug caused them. Violent personalities are usually found in those with identifiable genetic variations, and those we think of as morally degenerate were on that course well before they started using drugs. Blaming the drug, rather than individual personality and health issues has led us in the wrong policy direction. It's as if we outlawed the use of gasoline, on the basis that youngsters playing with matches might be injured by it. We know that in the wrong hands drugs can spell trouble, but so can many things.

Other substances and even activities result in addiction too. Food, sex and gambling are well known to become so salient as incentives in some people's lives as to meet the diagnostic criteria of addiction. We do not say that food or sex *cause* those addictions. Neither should we say drugs cause drug addiction. Drugs are simply the medium through which some addictions are manifest. Drug addiction affects about 10%–the vulnerable–who who use over prolonged periods.[125] In Chapter 7, we show that addiction occurs, not through chemical damage of the brain, but through a process identical to the way we learn useful things. Medical science has gone far beyond the old myths that drugs "fry" the brain, or turn normal people into "dope fiends."[126]

The use of drugs occurs not just among the underclasses, but among the seldom arrested affluent as well. You can find it among police personnel and public officials, Wall Street traders, nurses, physicians, ministers, accountants and so on through any occupation you can think of. Stressful situations and occupations are breeding grounds for substance disorders. Lawyers, for example face higher rates of depression and suicide—and substance disorders–than the wider population.[127] Most of these users function well, even expertly, whether their drug of choice is marijuana, heroin, cocaine or other drugs. Even those who are addicted often learn to manage their use effectively and live comparatively normal lives. The illegal drugs are even less likely to be involved in crime commission than alcohol. The National Commission on Alcoholism and Drug Dependence has reported that alcohol, more than any illegal drug, is associated with violent crimes, including murder, rape, assault, child and spousal abuse. Statistics related to alcohol use by violent offenders show that about half of all homicides and assaults are committed when the offender, victim, or both have been drinking. Among violent crimes, except for robberies, the offender is far more likely to have been drinking than under the influence of other drugs. Ironically, we do not ban alcohol use, though it leads to more crime and violence than any of the outlawed drugs.[128] Might it be that if we allowed adult drug use, we would actually reduce substance related crime? Some have argued this is a logical conclusion—that some would substitute drug use for the more problematic alcohol use.

Of course, abusive drug use and addiction are serious problems. I do not use drugs and I do not recommend anyone do so. The purpose of this chapter is to show that trying to address the ills involving them, with prohibition, is based on myth and misunderstanding. This is why it doesn't work. Uncluttered thinking about drug use and the causes and consequences of addiction will help speed us toward better solutions.

So why do myths and misunderstandings continue to have such power to influence policy, despite the evidence against them? Part of the answer lies in certain features of human nature.

Availability bias promotes acceptance of current punishment policies

For most of us, changing our thinking can be a challenge. You, I and everyone else are in the same boat we call human nature. The behavioral psychologists and behavioral economists have studied the way humans make decisions and judgments and offer many insights. One of those is called the availability bias. Their studies by researchers such as Daniel Kahneman show that we usually believe information most available to us, what we hear or read most frequently, though the evidence supporting it is weak.[129] Every day our news media publish accounts of drug related crimes. In these stories, the good guys are almost always the cops and the bad guys are drug users—we've been taught to think anyone who breaks the law is a bad guy. Drug users are law breakers and so must be bad. Most people are far too busy making a living, or raising kids, or getting an education to think this through and to challenge it with the scientific evidence available only by searching for it. And so, the readily *available* information shapes our thinking. It doesn't occur to us to think in a different way.

The researchers in behavior and decision-making have contributed greatly to our grasp of what causes us to behave and decide the way we do. Availability bias is at work continuously in the thinking of all of us. This feature of human nature and other heuristics, which go under various technical names such as confirmation bias and anchoring effects, go a long way toward explaining why we are resistant to evidence that conflicts with the beliefs we hold. The work of Dr. Kahneman is well worth reading by all who want to understand how bias shapes our thinking and conclusions.[130]

Overcoming bias with a focus on essential interests

In my training and work as a dispute mediator, I have seen up close the various biases at work and how major decisions stem from a mixture of both rational and emotional considerations. Often the emotional considerations crowd out the rational ones. Emotions helpfully augment reason, but should not displace it. Emotional responses play a role in drug policy. Think for example about the "war" analogy—one that is almost purely emotion based politician-speak. When we imagine the self-degradation of someone recklessly loading up on mind-altering substances, most of us feel a keen sense of disapproval. That is an emotional reaction consistent with the rational value we place on responsible conduct. When we witness it, we tend to turn away preferring not to see that wretched person. After all, we are not all social workers or other professionals able to view that same person through trained eyes. They see not a wretch, but a patient whose condition of addiction can be, and likely one day will be, successfully treated. The professional's emotional reaction is likely to be more along the sympathetic line, accompanied often by the joy of knowing how to help.

Unfortunately, perceptions among the rest of us are more likely tainted with an emotion- based prejudice–working against sound judgment in policy-making. Opinions, once formed, are seldom re-examined. Overcoming the effects of unexamined and erroneous opinion is only possible with accurate information in the context of important interests. This reality underlies the use in our legal system today of the process I referred to above—mediation—in which a neutral "mediator" helps the disputing parties communicate and negotiate more effectively. The mediator coaches the parties to focus on their true interests. By "true interests" I mean those things which are valuable to them in concrete ways, both for today and tomorrow, as distinguished from those that merely feel good, but make no substantial difference, such as getting revenge, punishing the other party, or proving a point of fact of no material importance. In evaluating a proposal and deciding whether to accept or reject it, parties are encouraged to examine trade-offs involving risks and rewards. The risk to a true interest might be the potentially costly loss of a lawsuit, or of a valuable relationship, or the prolongation of a troubled or wasteful situation. The mediator might ask a party to identify what is most important to him in the the process of negotiation. Is it proving the other party wrong? Teaching her a lesson? Getting revenge? Winning a monetary bonus? Or is it in the party's more important interest to avoid risk of monetary loss, or to correct an unwanted situation, or to salvage a valuable relationship? Looking at issues from the viewpoint of our important interests, even including important emotions, is a helpful way of arriving at the right decision.

In thinking this way about the drug laws, our truly important interests are (1) to protect our young from taking up harmful drug use, especially as that is where most drug use starts, (2) to rid our communities of the violence, crime and corruption of drug trafficking and dealing, and (3) to provide an optimal way for those already suffering a substance disorder to find a path toward responsible use, if not immediate sobriety. Those interests are not being realized under our laws against drugs. Yet, if we re-examine our opinions and take a fresh look at all the tools at our disposal for accomplishing those things, we find there is a way to do it. By re-framing the issue, we can think outside the constraints of our shop-worn opinions and envision the better way.

If we can re-focus our attention upon our more vital interests of keeping drugs away from the young, ending the violent and corrupting drug trade, helping addicts with a better pathway to recovery, then we can discover the talents and technologies available to us for accomplishing those objectives–and get on with them.

Unfortunately, there are influential interest groups who lobby politicians with promises of campaign support or threats of campaign opposition if they tinker with the laws against drugs. These may include beer manufacturers whose products compete with marijuana, unions of prison guards, whose jobs could be affected, and police departments where drug related money and property can be seized and used to supplement their budgets.

The problem of cognitive dissonance or "double-think"

Psychologists use the term cognitive dissonance to describe the situation in which a person holds an idea that conflicts with apparent realities–two conflicting beliefs at the same time. This seems to be a capability common to us all and with which we are seldom comfortable, though at a loss to know what to do about it. As I am not a psychologist, I will not press the point beyond raising this question: Given the more than four-decade failure of our drug war to accomplish its goals, might some of those who still favor prohibition be exhibiting cognitive dissonance?

In his popular novel "1984" George Orwell called it "double-think". In a book titled *Fear No Evil*, mathematician, holder of various cabinet posts in Israel and former Soviet dissident Natan Sharansky wrote of "double-think" defining it the same way: the human ability to hold two contradictory ideas at the same time. Sharansky has shown that living in the old Soviet Union, a fear based society, as he describes it, people professed the virtues of that repressive regime and suppressed contrary thoughts they knew were true, but thought to be socially and politically risky.

America is not a fear based society, but many parents do fear their children might take up drugs. And, despite a good deal of evidence to the contrary, there is a kind of public worry that tolerating adult drug use would usher in more crime and violence, and perhaps a dystopian society to boot. Under the weight of such worries, people can easily think it unwise to criticize the existing system, and simply accept the existing prohibition system as the only protection available. Even those aware of the many harmful consequences of the drug war may be more comfortable with the status quo than the controversial alternatives of legalization and decriminalization.

Double-think may stem from social risk–the uneasiness that comes with going against the grain of a group with whom an individual identifies. Writing for e-skeptic, Kenneth Krause explained this human foible: "Science—indeed, truth generally—is served mostly by those who conceive of themselves as individuals first and group members second (if at all). But seldom if ever are its ends advanced by committed disciples to any idea or cause." [131] When we comfortably belong to a group, there is a tendency to go along with what what we think is the shared view of the others. It is never comfortable to be a dissenter. Even holding a dubious belief may be more comfortable, because it conforms to the views of friends. It can be like popping a soothing pill. Of religion, Karl Marx famously said, "It is the opium of the people." I have great respect for people of religion and none for Marxian political thought, but the famous communist was right in thinking the humanly natural tendency to find comfort—even oblivion at times—lies in the tranquilizing effect of sharing a belief held by one's group.

When we depart from independent analysis and reach for the support of group belief, we set ourselves up for another human trait called confirmation bias. Comfortable with our peer supported belief, we astutely observe each bit of information supporting it and either fail to notice or consciously devalue information that contradicts it. This confirmation bias is at work in supporting our nation's drug policy. Progress in any quest for the right drug policy will be retarded for as long as too many of us fail to examine the science of drug abuse and addiction—and to re-examine why we are using criminal punishment where toleration and public health measures would serve better.

The phenomenon of double think is humanly natural. It occurs in the context of complex or misty ideas, where critical analysis is more difficult than the daily commonplace. Contrast a simple and absurd idea. If an authority proposed a new law that would legalize bank robberies there would be an instant and near universal rejection of such an idea as each of us realized it would undermine the banking services we depend on. Harm to our banks would harm us. However, we don't have such a clear and simple analysis when we confront the notion of removing drug use from the criminal punishment system; at least until we see a concrete and detailed idea that promises to work better. Criminalization of harmful conduct we wish to curtail has a long tradition. Steal: go to jail. Solicit prostitution: go to jail. Sell cigarettes to minors: pay a fine or go to jail. The laws against drug use were adopted in the belief that this kind of behavior, like any other, could be controlled and curtailed by the threat of criminal punishment. In this book, we see a concrete and detailed idea that promises to work far better.

The mistaken morality basis for current policy

As law and philosophy professor Douglas Husak points out, many deem drug use to be immoral and therefore a proper subject of prohibition.[132] But, this, he shows, does not follow. Our

Constitutional form of government was finalized in the context of the Declaration of Independence, which speaks of the self-evident truth that we are endowed with the right to life, liberty and the pursuit of happiness. It has not been our tradition to adopt prohibitive laws merely based on moral opinion. On the other hand, we do criminalize behaviors which harm others, and we often think of these as also immoral. But it is the fact of harm to others, not the immorality, that provides the clear constitutional basis for outlawing that behavior. In our legal system, we may not conduct ourselves in ways that deprive others of their right to life, liberty or pursuit of happiness. The traditional list of the "Seven Deadly Sins" includes wrath, greed, sloth, pride, lust, envy, and gluttony. None of those is enforced by law or punishment, except where the "sin" coincides with behavior that harms others. Greed may move a butcher's thumb onto the scale or induce a Willie Sutton to rob a bank, and so result in criminal sanctions, but no personal greed—unless it leads you to commit a crime that injures another–will land you in jail.

Interestingly, in a poll discussed by law professor Husak, 46% of the responders agreed *strongly* that drug use is immoral and should be prohibited. Another 15% agreed somewhat with that proposition while 17% said they "somewhat disagree" and 18% strongly disagreed. Now, Husak suggests, try to think of any other traditional crime such as robbery, rape, murder, burglary, and theft about which there is such a variance among people in their approval or disapproval of punishment. We nearly all agree on prohibition of behaviors that threaten the sanctity of life and property. According to the poll, we do not so agree about drug use. Since that early poll the Pew Research Center has done further polling on marijuana and found that most of us support legalizing its use.[133] We are punishing recreational users of drugs, though most of us are not at all sure we should do so. Seven states and the District of Columbia now legally permit the sale and use of marijuana for recreation and more are expected to follow suit.

The view that the responsible use of psychoactive drugs does not logically raise a morality issue enjoys scientific support in the observations reported by NIDA[134] and others that drug use and addiction relate to genetic and developmental problems, mostly in the young. It is also supported by surprising changes in the scientific thinking about other things we consume. For example, coffee, once thought to be bad for us, and still shunned by some religions, has been shown to reduce risks of heart attack and stroke. Used in moderation, it can help students learn by counteracting a brain neurotransmitter that inhibit the formation of new learning circuits. Alcohol is now medically approved as a healthy food for adults, when used moderately. Many may still think of it as "the devil's brew," but few would think we should go back to alcohol prohibition.

In recent years, churches have begun to solve their outreach problems by featuring social functions at which beer drinking is a main attraction. This was unthinkable not many years ago. A typical bottle of beer contains as much alcohol as a 4-ounce glass of wine or one ounce of 100-proof whiskey. Drink three or four beers over an hour and you are not fit by law to drive. Yet a Methodist church in Michigan, and a Catholic parish and several Episcopal churches in North Carolina and Texas, to mention a few, are using beer socials to attract young people to church sponsored gatherings. Pastors cite the long history of beer making in the church throughout Europe.[135] While those we look to for moral leadership have not widely come out in favor of legalizing drugs, some have. The Reverend Pat Robertson, once a Republican aspirant to the White House with a large religious following, has advocated the legalization of marijuana despite its availability in strengths much higher than in the 60s. Prohibitionists should ask themselves the question: what exactly is it about drugs that makes their use immoral even if only used in a moderate, responsible way?

For a very long time the public perception of immorality in drug use has been and continues to be promoted by AA and its 12-Steps. The organization was founded on the now disproved belief that drug use is immoral and punishes with the insanity of addiction. Science today shows something quite different. We examine the findings of science in Chapter 7. There we see that addiction is characterized by a craving that may be very difficult to resist, but it does not arise due to moral failure. The nerve cells (neurons) in our brains communicate with each other through neurotransmitters: chemicals that will carry the "message" as it moves from one nerve cell to the next. Principally, dopamine is the neurotransmitter producing feelings of well-being, reduction of fear and anxiety, and promotion of emotional balance. If taking a drug stimulates an excess production of dopamine it heightens the pleasurable effects of the drug and may transmit a strong signal to take it again—and then again—and repeat. This is especially so for those who suffer anxiety or emotional imbalance. These are the people vulnerable to addiction and for them the opiates are medicine. It is not an ecstatic high they seek, but merely relief from psychic pain.

In his book "Drug Crazy," Mike Gray offers a way to understand the mind of a drug addict.[136] Suppose, he imagines, there were suddenly a government ban on food. Over a couple of days, you might fare okay, but after that you would think of nothing else but food and how to get it. A black market would spring up and you would be able to buy a hot dog, but now it could cost you $50. When your money runs out, you would be likely to consider stealing food even money to buy it with. I don't intend to suggest drug craving is the same as going hungry. But the idea that drug addiction, a condition in which choice is constrained,[137] is a matter of bad character is also false. In the next chapter, we'll see it's relation to the processes of learning and the work of incentives and cues, which can trap the young and vulnerable person into addiction, until he or she learns how to change brain circuits in a pathway to health.

Young people with attention deficit hyperactivity disorder (ADHD), a condition diagnosed in about 13% of boys and about 6% of girls, [138] are considered, as we noted in Chapter 3, to have an increased vulnerability to drug use and addiction. Other genetic and developmental problems also contribute. And as previously discussed, most adult addiction begins with childhood experimentation. How can we morally condemn addicts for cravings gone beyond their control, which started in adolescence, due mostly to a vulnerability they could not have prevented?

Understanding the relation of vulnerability and adolescence to addiction, how can we think of addiction compelled drug taking as criminal? We don't condemn mentally ill persons for aberrant behavior resulting from the illness and we certainly do not criminalize them. If we are a humane people, and there is little doubt we are, we cannot and do not fault people for behaviors induced by a disorder beyond their control.

As Volkow, et. al., point out, adolescence is a time in life where vulnerability to addiction is most likely to be manifest. Adolescents are true dynamists, not bound by tradition and static thinking. They are all about experimenting, adventuring, and having fun. On the other hand, they are also often at risk of depression and anxiety, for this is a time of brain and bodily changes, competing pressures and social tensions and confusions. Drug use pleasures are a motivating attraction to some, but there are additional motivators. It can seem an entirely benign form of pleasure, and it can relieve symptoms of depression and anxiety. Motivated repetition leads to addiction.[139] We need to develop a system that helps prevent youthful onset of drug use for the sake of their better education and development. And we need to drop the pointless moralizing.

On the broad issue of morality, the reckless or irresponsible use of drugs is another matter. Getting behind the wheel of a car while drug or alcohol impaired is immoral, because it raises the risk of injury to others. Teenagers know this law is designed for the physical safety of of others. We make it a crime, not because it is immoral, but because it is unsafe for everyone on the road. Other examples where drug use is associated with immorality because it harms others include neglecting a child while intoxicated and working with hazardous equipment while in a drowsy state induced by marijuana or heroin. Under the system proposed, criminal penalties would continue to apply when irresponsible drug use results in harm to others.

The "burden on society" rationale for prohibition

Irresponsible drug use nearly always impairs good judgment and desirable behaviors. Drug abusers become unproductive, fail in their responsibilities, cause family breakups and more. Excessive use may lead to illness and add to the strain of high medical costs across the nation. A major reason we ban drugs, it is said, is to avoid the health care costs and social disruptions drug abuse and addiction sometimes entail. Abuse and addiction burden us all, if only indirectly, but can we square our pursuit of drug prohibition with our toleration of so many things that are just as bad or worse?

Examples include risky eating behaviors and alcohol use. Sugar and high-fructose corn syrup (and pizza and cake) are said to be as addicting as cocaine, and they lead to obesity and diabetes, yet we do not control their use. Obesity and diabetes have major social consequences, especially in health care costs, and over-eating is far more prevalent than drug abuse. Only about 7% of us use illegal drugs. How many in the U.S. are obese? According to the Centers for Disease Control and Prevention, 35.7% are obese and therefore at risk of diabetes. Yet, we do not, and should not, attempt to protect people from their own poor eating habits with threats of arrest and jail. Alcohol abuse results in family breakups and other social ills, vastly worse than drug use, yet we do not punish the doctor who maintains an extensive wine cellar or the executive who enjoys a three-martini lunch, or any of the millions who stop in at a saloon after work and get a little high with friends before heading for home.

The System proposed is neither liberal nor conservative, but dynamistic in nature

Thoughtful and honest people stand in the ranks of both the major political philosophy camps in the U.S. Liberals and conservatives can both embrace the dynamism of a system that harnesses legal market forces to defeat black market crime and corruption. The Global Commission on Drug Policy, cited above, consists of people representing the full spectrum of political thought. Public intellectuals of all stripes support ending our pursuit of prohibition.

The defining characteristic of dynamism is its willingness to try new methods to solve problems, not in a reckless way, but in a way that tries to evaluate the likelihood of success based upon historical experience, current information and rational thought. Dynamists have always been the engine of our industrial power and its creatively destructive economy, regardless of whether they called themselves liberal or conservative or libertarian or some other "ist" or "ian." Dynamists welcome change, trial and error, experimentation and innovation and prefer a continuous reexamination of what might make a better world. They embrace the "creative destruction" that economist Joseph Schumpeter showed is a necessary pre-condition for progress in the development of man's greatest potential.

In her book The *Future and its Enemies, The Growing Conflict over Creativity, Enterprise and Progress,* former Reason Magazine editor and author Virginia Postrel makes a compelling case for allowing the energy of dynamism to shape our future, through learning and innovation. She warns that frequently reactionary resistance to change can dim the brightness of our future. While Postrel's book does not address the issues of drug policy, it shows the vitality of the very same kind of dynamic innovation the System proposed offers and compellingly argues for change especially when the old ways are so destructive. The new System would harness the forces of a free market, align with various aspects of predictable human behavior, and trust to those in the field, motivated by the potential for career success, the counselors, to find the best practices for fostering responsible drug use by adults. It does not exclude scholarly and expert guidance, but nor does it assume that all the knowledge of what will be needed must come from those sources. The dynamist is one who looks for opportunities to let the free agents in the world make things happen according to the preferences of the many, allowing corrections and adjustments as experience dictates along the way. Proposed changes in the way things are done should always reflect careful analysis, but dynamists embrace well-considered change.

Hear the voices of some prominent dynamists.

Former Democratic Secretary of the Treasury Robert Rubin: "The goal of policy in the coming century should be to encourage rather than suppress competition and innovation...." *Washington Post* columnist, David Ignatius: "... (the global economy is) a dynamic, complex, adaptive system that is constantly adapting to changing circumstances." Martin Luther King had a similar take: "There is little hope for us until we become tough minded enough to break loose from the shackles of prejudice, half-truths and downright ignorance... A nation or a civilization that continues to produce soft minded men purchases its own spiritual death on an installment plan."[140] Nobel Prize economist and philosopher Friedrich Hayek described dynamism as "the party of life, the party that favors free growth and spontaneous evolution." Nobel Prize economist Edmund S. Phelps said: "I argue that high dynamism is essential for the good life.... This ... is in a line that starts with Aristotle and runs through the vitalists such as Cellini, Cervantes, William James and Henri Bergson and runs also through the pragmatists such as Virgil, John Dewey and Amartya Sen."[141]

The concept of dynamism is key to the thinking that will drive the proposed System, and, in its adoption, the experience that will lead us toward a drug responsible world. Both conservatives and liberals can come together to make this happen in drug policy reform.

The system and creative destruction

In adopting the System, we would embrace Schumpeter's great insight he called creative destruction. Though the System will inevitably, if only slowly, reduce the need for prison guards, prison construction workers, and law enforcement personnel, it will create an engine for job creation and opportunities for all those displaced workers. Counselors, office managers and clerical workers and warehouse people will be needed—eventually in vast numbers. It will also produce jobs ranging from packaging and mailing, and back office staff, to professional counselors and monitors, and business managers. Even college liberal arts students with a generalized education make good candidates. They often have difficulty finding good paying jobs because their education was not specialized, but a liberal education with its emphasis on critical thinking, communication skills, and ability to master new subjects well equips the graduate to serve, following a brief training. Such an education likely provides the best foundation for life, and liberal arts students become excellent role models.[142]

Operation of this system would be outside federal and state bureaucracies and would enjoy the flexibility to experiment and innovate with broad goals and objectives in mind. There is a role for government to play but it is not in the operation of the System. Governmental oversight will be as important as traffic cops in the urban downtown, but bureaucrats are not good at doing business. Private entrepreneurs and venture capitalists, or in different models the officers of non-profit corporations or enterprise districts, accountable for successful operation, can efficiently employ thousands of people in each state choosing to implement the System.

A second and even more valuable form of creative destruction will be the end of the black market. The System's feature of legal drug dispensing will invoke market forces, the most robust and irresistible forces there are, to kill the drug trade that makes millionaires of crooks, and spawns the tens of thousands of small-scale dealers and the thousands of gangs who deliver these substances to our young people.

The end of the need for arresting and imprisoning responsible drug users and the drop in acquisitive crimes by addicts will free up resources all the better to discourage violent crime; interdict any residual illegal drug flow; and prosecute those traffickers and dealers who may try to continue in an unprofitable underground market. It should be expected, however, that because it will take time for the System to reach its potential, any reduction in law enforcement jobs will occur only gradually and mainly through attrition. Police officers and prison guards need not fear for their careers.

The manufacturers of alcoholic beverages may fear the effects of competition with drugs. This worry is said to be already manifest in the lobbying by beer companies against legalization of marijuana. Under legalization marijuana would be a cheaper high than beer and might drive down brewers' sales. While I doubt beer will ever have trouble competing with marijuana, there is no reason we should protect the brewers from free enterprise creative destruction. Free enterprise will continue to make their work profitable.

Chapter 7:

Reducing Addiction through Prevention and Recovery

Human behavior flows from three main sources: desire, emotion, and knowledge.

Plato

Addiction Prevention

The prevention of new addictions among the young, currently estimated at near 200,000 per year is perhaps the most salient promise of the new System. To appreciate this, you should first know that about 80% of the U.S. drug purchases are made by adults.[143] It is the over-21 demand for drugs that makes the illegal drug trade so profitable, putting hundreds of thousands of gangs, small-scale dealers and user/dealers pervasively into the neighborhoods, where adolescents can access them–and they can access adolescents. Our adult use tolerant System, I detail in Chapter 8, ends that trade and access and stops much of the adolescent addiction problem in its tracks. How does that work?

System control mechanisms both reduce and help prevent addiction.

While it is the adult demand that fuels the illegal drug trade, addiction occurs mostly among adolescents, the age of greatest vulnerability to addiction. CASA has done a robust examination of the literature and data, and concluded that 90% of the addicted got their start with drugs during ages 12 through 17.[144] Of course, age 18 is no cutoff date. The adolescent brain is not complete until anywhere from six to twelve years later. Addictions form among users 18 and older, but just at a progressively slower rate as we go up the age scale. Young people get drugs often from family medicine chests, but also from the pervasive small-scale dealers and gangs plying their trade in every community and near every high school.

According to surveys, 44% of high school students know someone who has sold drugs at school. The drugs reported were 91% marijuana, 24% prescription drugs, 9% cocaine and 7% ecstasy. About 52% of high school students knew of a place on school grounds or near school where students use drugs, as well as drink and smoke, and 36% said it was easy to use drugs at school without getting caught. About 75% of 12-to-17-year-olds had seen pictures of teens partying with alcohol or marijuana on Facebook or other social media, and were encouraged to party like that, while 47% of those who saw these pictures said that it seemed like the teens shown in the pictures were having a good time.[145]

Most teenagers know that often misinformation and even nonsense is mixed with what adults tell them about the dangers of drugs. They notice that members of their age group, and younger and older ones too, smoke pot or meth with no apparent damage. Most of them heed the warnings of their parents and teachers and so remain drug free. That is because most have stronger personal resources and look ahead to productive life. But more than a quarter of them will begin regular drug-taking out of rebellion or in a quest for adventure or escapism. What they can't know is to what extent they may be vulnerable. Teen years are the time of psychological, social and biological changes that lead to emotional turmoil from which drugs may offer relief. Brain development, especially the prefrontal cortex, where self-regulation resides, may take all the first three decades of life.[146] Drug experimentation and continued use by some should be expected, because it makes life more bearable. Here is how a 19- year-old college student described his experience:

> The world is all messed up…. When I'm high, I can take things better. Before I came to…college, I felt home life was one great big mess; now that I'm here, this college is also a big pile of crap. I guess that is why I like smoking dope. When I'm high I can forget my problems.[147]

This young person is in danger of making a habit of preferring escape from problems, rather than solving them. Some construct their social world with friends who use drugs. Here are the words of a 21-year-old college student:[148]

> I have been using drugs since I was 12 years old. Nearly all of my best friends are like me [in using drugs]. We just don't hang around with people who are against or afraid to use drugs…. People say you can't learn or study while on drugs. For me, I do everything when I am high on weed. If I have homework to do I probably do waste more time when I am high, but I still get the work done…. After a few years of first using drugs, most normal people learn how to live their life around drug use. You learn when it's too much and learn how not to overdo a particular drug. I know there are many drug users who don't learn very well, but that's an individual thing. Actually, I know more people who use drugs wisely (most of the time) and really don't have a problem. On the other hand, they may have a problem for a while, but learn from their mistakes.

This relating of drug use to a social life helps maintain the habit. One of the powerful "cues" we discuss in Chapter 7 that trigger drug wanting is the presence of friends with whom pleasurable use was enjoyed. The young man's comment that most "normal" people learn not to overdo is borne out by research data, but he is likely fooling himself in thinking there are no hazards to his learning and his future. He also confirms another fact–some individuals may not be able to "learn from their mistakes." Those are the ones who may not have strengths he is endowed with.[149]

Another college student told the interviewer that he had been at least a little high nearly always through high school. Now in college and continuing to smoke weed, he has a B+ or higher average in all his classes as a psychology major. He too avoids socializing with people who are against drugs.[150] According to the researchers who obtained these interviews they reflect the beliefs and behaviors of many young people who got their start with drugs as adolescent.

The System's control measures have several purposes, but the most important of these is preventing addiction by keeping drugs out of the hands of minors. I summarize them here:

1. As we've seen, as drugs are dispensed to adult users through a narrow channel of distribution, the availability of drugs to minors is decreased as the various peddlers and their suppliers leave town, or go out of business.

2. Clients purchase only predetermined amounts sufficient to use over specified time intervals. Due to this limitation, they are unlikely to be willing to share their drugs with others including minors. Clients agree to periodic, random blood/drug checks, more frequently at the beginning, to facilitate determination that only the authorized drug is being used and in the quantities agreed upon. Too little in the blood would raise suspicion the client is selling to or sharing with others. Too much invites a conversation about bingeing. Violations might result in supply reductions,

more frequent testing, shortened purchase intervals, etc. Attempts to buy more than the agreed amount or outside the agreed intervals would raise immediate suspicion of cheating. If a client loses his interval's supply, he will have to speak with his counselor about an emergency replacement. If a counselor suspects the claim is not an innocent one, measures might be taken such as more frequent monitoring or stricter limitations.

3. Applicants sign a contract which among other things commits them to take all reasonable precautions against access to their drugs by others, especially minors. Clients are warned that if law enforcement finds drugs in someone else's possession traceable back to them, a violation would be presumed. Both ouster from the program and a criminal prosecution are potential consequences.

4. Clients of the System are screened at intake and their living arrangements noted so the assigned counselor can prescribe measures to avoid leakage of the drugs to children and others. The home may be investigated and the client asked to show how she will lock up the drug against pilfering. Absent a satisfactory showing, the client may be required to take the drug only at a designated consumption sites.

These and perhaps other measures would be the natural controls in a system designed to protect against leakage of drugs into the wrong hands. Perfection is not to be expected and there will be violations, but access of drugs by minors will certainly be curtailed.

Prevention of addiction also occurs in the System by means of another important function of the counselors: that of educating their clients. As we have noted repeatedly in this book the clear majority of regular drug users do not fit the criteria for drug addiction. It is certainly not the case, however, that all non-addicted users will avoid eventual addiction. All users of these drugs who engage in prolonged use, and have a vulnerability to addiction, are at risk. The trained counselors make all pertinent scientific information available to their clients and this includes not just the properties of the drugs dispensed, but the science of addiction as well. No, they don't teach neuroscience, but they are armed with helpful science-based information. By these means, the risk of addiction among the myopic and vulnerable groups can be reduced in many cases and for some eliminated entirely.

As to those already addicted the System promotes recovery. Let's see how that works.

ADDICTION RECOVERY

As we have seen, most addiction strikes the young in a kind of developmental setback and that they mature out by their early thirties. Some severe addictions, often accompanied by a co-occurring mental disorder require intervention by treating professionals, while most with any level of substance use disorders quit on their own. Yet, because successful rehab requires a high level of readiness and commitment, many go into treatment and fail, sometimes repeatedly over many attempts.

Addiction treatment can be and often is expensive. Its coverage under national health care policies is not assured. Nor is successful rehab likely for those who are not yet ready to do the demanding work of self-regulation. The counselors in the System proposed do not offer treatment, but the coaching and guiding toward responsible use they do provide will take their clients a long way toward recovery–setting up a platform, so to say, from which they climb to wellness is shorter and easier. To bring these facts into sharper relief, the following is an overview of the science of addiction.

The nature of addiction and its implications for recovery

Modern science offers strong foundational support for the System I propose. This is so because every aspect of the System helps move those with substance disorders along a healthful pathway. Several factors work to speed the addicted toward recovery. Keep these in mind as we discuss the modern understanding of addiction.

- Stress reduction and stabilization. While stress is not a prime cause of addiction, it is a characteristic condition of it. Using drugs has become the way the addict copes. A person whose entire focus is on getting and paying for drugs, often lying to others to evade detection, maybe stealing from medicine cabinets, and even committing crimes to pay for drugs, lives an unstable, stress-filled life: one larded with cues that trigger drug wanting. When relieved of the stress and near constant preoccupation with drugs, the life of the addicted is more stable: they can stretch periods of abstinence and find more time and ways to strengthen the personal resources they need to conquer their habits.
- Avoidance of cues. Through changing environments and associations, the addicted reduce the frequency of their feelings of need for the drug.
- New opportunities and incentives. These provide alternative motivations. For the addict, the drug has become the most salient incentive, making it difficult to even think of alternative ways of living. Social interaction promotes the formation of new self-identity and healthier incentives.
- Informed understanding of the problem. The addicted think of themselves as entrapped in a habit from which they can't escape. Accurate information shows them there is a way out of addiction: that not only is escape possible, it is usual.

Various writers who discuss the scientific research, often disagree on some details, but we nevertheless have a coherent body of thought and a far clearer picture of addiction than ever before.

One point of disagreement is whether we should call addiction a disease. The research organization NIDA, states that addiction is a "chronic relapsing disease of the brain." Others argue it should be called a disorder, because it differs so widely from what we normally think of as disease. The Volkow paper. cited earlier, strongly urges us to stick with the disease model. Addiction is a disease, the authors say, because it involves changes in the structures of the brain; it is a self-destructive behavior; medicines are helpfully used in rehab treatment; and a treatment method called contingency management (offering incentives to abstain) is also used in medical treatments, for example to motivate the sick to take better care of themselves. Besides, they contend, the disease model reduces stigma and promotes addiction treatment and insurance coverage, because it disarms the moralists–the prohibitionists who support criminal punishment.[151]

The dissenters argue the disease model is misleading to the addicted about the pathway to sobriety, because it makes them feel helpless without treatment, contrary to reality. They suggest the real motive for the disease model dating back to the 1990's was advanced to promote government funding for research.[152] Calling addiction a disease, makes addiction research sound medical and therefore more interesting to politicians. Politicians are always up for promoting advances in medical science. An early head of NIDA admitted calling addiction a disease was a "Faustian bargain," which overlooks important aspects of the problem.[153]

Psychologist and addiction expert Gene Heyman has studied and written about addiction for over two decades. He points out there is no condition we think of as disease, which the sufferer can terminate by choosing to do so. You can't get rid of the proteins that cause Alzheimer's by changing your thoughts and behaviors. He shows data proving the fact, not denied by the NIDA scientists, that most people with addiction terminate it on their own without treatment—by doing just that. He concedes drug habits can be difficult to quit, and for some impossible,[154] but argues that seldom is self-control lost altogether–the addict retains the choice of quitting.

Still, whatever motivates the insistence that addiction is a disease, the word is ingrained in the medical and the political vocabulary and not likely to be abandoned. In the information- rich System I propose, the counselors make sure their clients understand the pathway to recovery, free of misconceptions of helplessness without medical treatment.

Treatment specialist Marc Lewis emphasizes the motivated repetition of drug taking as key to addiction. He speaks of the biology of desire. The pleasure response and relief of discomfort motivate repetition. A positive emotion is generated in place of the negative, when the drug brings pleasure or relieves a discomfort. Joining in the rejection of the disease model, Lewis says: "Addiction is unquestionably destructive, yet it is also uncannily normal: an inevitable feature of the basic human design," and he goes on to insist: "the brain changes with addiction. But the way it changes has to do with learning and development—not disease."[155]This exact point was made by Satel and Lilienfeld in their earlier book, *Brainwashed.* [156] The point is based on solid scientific research.

And it provides the key to addiction recovery. What we learn can be unlearned or at least over-written, somewhat like the way we overwrite a hard drive.

Neuroscientist, Alex Korb agrees. He explains that addictions start as "pleasurable impulses." But, as use continues, the brain's reward centers eventually stop responding and the pleasure diminishes and disappears. Yet, the learned response to the drug, a kind of rewiring, remains and the addicted feel compelled to use again, even though they don't expect pleasure.[157] The habit is ingrained in the part of the brain separate from the regions involved with self-control or regulation. And, as Lewis states, self-control is weakened at the same time the habit is strengthened.[158] To regain control, addicts must rebuild strength in the prefrontal cortex to increase self-regulation. We might think of it as being like going to the gym to rebuild muscles gone weak from disuse. And, as Korb explains, this can be hard to do under stress, because stress activates a person's coping habits. If using a drug is how the person copes with life challenges, stress takes her right back to the drug, pleasure or no pleasure. Then this promotes more stress and a feedback loop is in place.

Addiction experts often describe drug taking as a form of self-medication. Users are motivated to take the drug because it helps them cope with their depression, anxiety, pain or some other emotional imbalance. Life without the drug for them would be unbearable. Addiction starts, they say, with a vulnerability stemming from early childhood experiences or physical conditions that interfere with development later during the adolescent years. It is during those turbulent teenage years, when social challenges accompany dynamic changes occurring in the developing brain that addiction forms. Adolescents will often, out of rebellion or impulsive adventurism, try a drug. And then, discovering it takes away their social anxiety or feeling of inferiority, or some other stress, they use it again—and again—and again. The pleasure response to the drug begins with a beguiling deception and then delivers addiction, instead of a happier life.

The paper by Volkow, et. al., cited earlier, supports this view. They explain that only certain vulnerable people—the developmentally challenged—make up the 10% or so of users who fall prey to addiction. The journalist Maia Szalavitz expresses this also in her book *Unbroken Brain,* which details her childhood condition resembling mild autism, which kept her in a state of social isolation.[159] Her story of heroin addiction exemplifies the point made by treating specialist Gabor Maté.[160] Addictions can be traced back to emotional imbalances, which likely developed in consequence of early childhood troubles. It is not a chemically induced euphoria that keeps the addicts going back for more, he explains, but the need to medicate the emotional pain—anxiety, depression--they suffer. Of course, drug use was the wrong choice of remedies to begin with, but the young are not always among the wisest in making choices, especially when developmental problems make life extra difficult.

Progress toward recovery involves developing both the motivation to succeed and the belief it is possible. In opposing the use of the word disease to describe addiction, Satel and Lilienfeld argue it works against this understanding, teaching the addicted a distorted view of their problem.[161] It encourages them to hold false notions about how their recovery might occur–to think maybe the day will come when a brain surgeon will be able to go in with a scalpel and carve out the diseased part, or with other shiny instruments poke around and rearrange things to take away the drug craving. Or the addict decides to just wait for a new pill that could do the same. This was the thinking that prolonged Hal's addiction long after he first wanted to quit. No easy medical solution is likely on its way and that is probably a very good thing. Anyone whose limbic system is so altered might also stop caring about sex, or enjoying ice cream, or a cold beer on a hot day at the ballpark. We need our brain's reward system for a lot of reasons, including survival of our species.

Through informed and motivated thinking–positive use of the mind–the brain can change itself for the better. Counselors in the System would make sure their clients understand that.

Putting it another way, the brain circuits, arranged for addiction by the motivated repetition process, can be rearranged in the same way. The scientists call this neuroplasticity of the brain—its ability to change. And this is done, not by treating the brain with chemicals or instruments, but by changing the individual's own thinking, usually aided by changes in behaviors as well. The brain undergoes a "re-wiring" of the circuits temporarily gone, well, haywire. The person's self-awareness and incentive appreciation are rewired.

This is not just theory, folks, though many of us were taught as late as about 1965 to think the mature brain is unchangeable. Neuroscientists and psychologists have proved beyond doubt: the brain has a marvelous capacity to change itself through conscious thought and choice. It changes for the better when, among other things, occupied in envisioning a healthy, productive and happier future. These new incentives compete with the drug for salience. In stages, a new self-identity forms and self-regulation—the control over emotions exercised by the prefrontal cortex–strengthens. The disordered brain is returning to its natural state–naturally. Szalavitz speaks of recovery from addiction as a positive development process, taking the person to an even higher level of personal strength than if there had been no addiction. This makes sense, because the addicted who recover, have worked hard to build more mental muscle. They "went to the gym" and got their brains in shape. In the exercise of new thinking and behavior, somewhat in the way a sickly Teddy Roosevelt challenged himself physically and became famously robust, they have built themselves into stronger, wiser persons.

This self-healing property of the brain is in many cases aided by medically assisted treatment or "MAT." MAT does not cure addiction, but as Volkow, et. al note, it is a most helpful treatment. Medicines such as methadone and buprenorphine give the addict space to work on developing a better mindset. Doctors administer the medicines once a day, eliminating the need to shoot up several times during the day. They imitate the opioids, but without the craving or withdrawal symptoms. They serve to help patients change living patterns, quit stealing to buy drugs, for example, and avoid other situations in which cues trigger drug wanting. They stabilize their lives by functioning more normally. That stabilization can be the first step in which they might develop new incentives that compete with drugs and seek effective rehab or just quit.

Cues that trigger drug wanting abound in the lives of the addicted, in the environment in which they live and work and internally in their memories. Satel and Lilienfeld tell of a school teacher addicted to cocaine who had to change out her blackboard and chalk with a whiteboard and marker. The chalk dust reminded her of powder cocaine and started her craving.

For one in addiction, the mere thought of the drug triggers the pleasure response and starts the brain's dopamine production. The dopamine flows to its natural receptor neurons and the brain takes over, shutting down the control center and opening the emotional and action centers to direct the drug seeking. Lights, camera, action! As Maté points out, the decision to take the drug is near instantaneous. Mindfulness training is being used to help patients slow that thought/decision interval down so the addict has a chance to slip in a more constructive thought or two and postpone reaching for the drug.

We are moving, here, toward the explanation of how the System I propose promotes the healthy pathway toward addiction recovery. First, let's return to the point made earlier about incentives. The experts all agree: drug users respond to incentives. A negative incentive such as staying out of jail sometimes works for those on probation to quit their habits. The power of *positive* incentives has also been shown in research by Hart, and others. Hart's addicted subjects could pass up a free "hit" of meth or cocaine for as little as a five-dollar bill.[162]

The government sponsored study of the heroin addicted Vietnam veterans offers a vivid example of the power of incentives, when cues are reduced. An eminent researcher, Lee Robins and colleagues studied hundreds of cases, years after the end of the war. The Nixon administration had mandated that veterans ending their tour of duty had to pass a blood test before they could embark for home. Motivated by the desire to get home, they passed their blood tests. On returning home, motivated by the incentives of good jobs and young families to raise, the majority quit on their own without relapsing. Of those who did relapse after returning home, most still achieved complete and permanent abstinence, some with and some without treatment. They were well away from the environment in which they had come to depend on heroin, and new incentives awaited them stateside. Both the cues and the incentives for these people had changed and they quit the drug.[163] Other large-scale studies have shown comparable results: incentives shape behavior. This means that for most addicts "treatment" may be unnecessary. "Recovery is a project of the heart and mind. The person, not his or her autonomous brain, is the agent of recovery."[164] Motivated addicts can get drug free on their own and many do so.

In Vietnam, these people were subjected to the stresses of boredom, anxiety and sometimes terror. Some found it easier to cope by using heroin. At home, for some, stressful situations sent them back to heroin. But, the old cues—places where and pals with whom heroin was taken, and the other environmental features that triggered drug wanting—were behind them. Now a changed environment, with new opportunities, both economic and social, provided different incentives. Only a few found coping with stresses, without the drug, too difficult to quit it.

The System promotes the pathway to recovery

Three important changes helped in the recovery success of the addicted returning veterans. Stress levels were reduced once they were removed from the terrors and the boredom that tortured them in Vietnam; they had left behind the cue-rich environment where they had been using heroin; and new opportunities and incentives lay before them back home as they returned to or started families and embarked on employment careers. Changes of a similar sort can occur too in a drug tolerant system that removes the stresses of getting and paying for drugs along with the over-hanging threat of incarceration; eliminates some of the external and internal cues that trigger drug wanting; and with the counseling component helps addicts envision opportunities and healthy incentives.

In Chapter 3, we saw that a by-product of harm reduction programs such as needle exchanges and diversion programs is the boost they give to an addict's self-esteem. A small amount of respect can often serve as the start of Korb's "upward spiral." We have also learned a good deal from the 12-Step method, even if what we have learned is not entirely complimentary to it.

The 12-Step method has provided six decades of experience and is widely practiced among the great majority of treating clinics. Fletcher shows it has become a convenient vehicle in the treating industry for processing people through a "one size fits all" program, contrary to the need for most addicts for individualized treatment. Based on what we have learned of the complexity of addiction, Fletcher argues, this approach is a set-up for failure.[165] Instead of teaching the power within each of us to change our brains, AA and its narcotic drug cousin, NA insist addiction is permanent. By their lights, one should not hope to attain healing, but accept that addiction is a lifetime disease against which one must struggle for a lifetime. Data collections show the drop-out rate of those who start with a 12-step group is great, and that among those who stay, relapse is frequent.

Such a discouraging message doesn't work for many. Persuading addicts to believe they cannot quit without the help of a 12-Step group or treating professional works against recovery as it promotes a passive leave-it-to-others attitude. Success entails doing the challenging work of avoiding cues and strengthening self-regulation. Lacking better information, addicts may assume they are hopelessly diseased and so only others can help them. They may come to formal rehab with a "here I am, fix me" attitude, but with little willingness to undertake the demanding work of change. Lewis tells of a "rigorous" study indicating the only pretreatment characteristic predicting relapse six months after outpatient treatment for alcoholism was the extent to which subjects believed in the disease model. Peele and Szalavitz both oppose that model and emphasize that the tenets of AA and NA are not supported in the scientific evidence.

Still, the method has helped many, and from those successes we have learned some valuable lessons that can be applied by program counselors in our new System, not to treat, but as part of their responsible use coaching. As a by-product, the program helps its clients stabilize their lives and change their focus toward healthier incentives.

Szalavitz writes that in her group, she enjoyed meeting with others with similar problems and experiences. There she felt accepted and valued. She found it comforting to be with a group of other struggling with similar problems and realized she was not a freak after all. Yet, she suggests her success in quitting may have been *despite* the treatment she received.[166] She allows that her AA sponsor had helped her in her self-reflection. The 12 Step programs "don't get everything wrong" she says. Lewis suggests the same. He quotes one recovering addict as saying: "I have completed the steps – however, I see them as steppingstones rather than a Solution."[167]

Through observations of the 12-Step groups and rehab services using 12-Step it is clear that an ingredient important for success in treatment is the motivation to stay with the program. Those who succeed have discovered in themselves the power to restore self-control and to form a healthy self-awareness—and worked at doing that. They had motivation, likely due to envisioning a better life or finding a goal to pursue, the way Navy Seal Adam Brown did.

In a study conducted in New York City between May 2001 and January 2002 where the data collected were from patients and clinicians both primarily of African-American and Hispanic heredity, and the drugs of choice were crack and marijuana, researchers concluded:

> Both staff and clients viewed 12SG (12 Step group) as a helpful recovery resource. Major obstacles to participation centered on motivation and readiness for change and on perceived need for help, rather than on aspects of the 12-step program often cited as points of resistance (e.g., religious aspect and emphasis on powerlessness)."[168]

The importance of the mindset and motivation of the patient is also stressed by Peele, who sharply criticizes 12-Step treatment, especially when it is coerced.[169] Coercion may be in the form of a drug court order or at the insistence of an employer, a partner or a spouse. Forced into 12-Step before they are ready for treatment--before they have found any motivation to quit--often results in discouraging failure.

Peele supports his argument with survey data, however, in a personal interview, two Superior Court judges who preside over drug courts, told me they have been pleased with the success achieved in sending probationers to treatment. In their opinions, coercion does not predict failure.[170] This view is supported by addiction expert Heyman, and policy expert Mark Kleiman. Both point to data showing the threat of a sure and swift, though comparatively mild, punishment provides a useful incentive to probationers to complete ordered treatment and remain abstinent.[171] Kleiman also acknowledges, however, that many of those sent to treatment by the court drift off and do not complete the program.[172] And, as noted elsewhere, drug courts see only a very small fraction of the addicted.

Thomas G. Brown, an assistant professor of psychiatry at McGill University, refers to: "a factor that may be important in potentiating A.A.'s benefits, namely patient choice and preference." The importance of patient choice is an insight researchers and practitioners in the field often emphasize.[173] One purpose of the System's counseling component is to assure clients are provided information to make well-informed choices among the various treatment methods.

The research of Dr. Edward Nunes, professor of psychiatry at Columbia, has supported the claim that certain elements of A.A. are effective. The benefit of avoiding cues that trigger drug wanting are taught there as in cognitive-behavioral therapy, "a scientifically driven, empirically validated treatment,"[174] John F. Kelly, a clinical psychologist at Harvard, said A.A. and other 12 Step programs "are not cure-alls, but I would say at a minimum, they help."[175]

A 2006 study at the Italian Agency for Public Health in Rome, suggested 12 Step interventions are no more or less successful in treating alcohol addiction than any of several other forms of treatment including cognitive-behavioral therapy, which encourages the conscious identification of high-risk situations (cues) for alcohol use; motivational enhancement therapy, based on principles of social and cognitive psychology (focus on incentives); and relapse prevention therapy.[176]

So, it appears 12-Step groups do help some and that they do it by offering three elements of treatment important to recovery–social interaction and feeling of acceptance; learning to avoid cues that trigger the wanting or craving; and working to rebuild the brain's capacity for self-control. Notice that each and all of these are integral to the System's teaching of responsible drug use.

The insistence of 12-Step upon abstention may, however, explain why the method fails so many. As we noted earlier, abstinence for one not yet ready to abstain can be a counterproductive source of stress. Fletcher shows in her book that a great deal of time and money are wasted on treatment methods and clinics by addicts who are uninformed or misinformed about how recovery occurs and the best treatment options for the individual. What works for some does not work for others.[177]   She quotes prominent researcher

Mark Sobell: "…specialty services are not appropriate for persons with problems that are not severe. And often those services are not appropriate for people whose problems *are* severe."[178]

In an earlier chapter I talked about Hal, who, like so many, left his 12-Step group, but later succeeded on his own to quit his meth habit. Fletcher tells a similar story. Sam D., as she calls her subject, had become addicted to painkillers and refused to accept the advice of a doctor who told him his only hope was rehab. Later, another doctor told him he would never succeed without group treatment, but Sam had already made up his mind to quit. Strongly committed to recovery after years of addiction, he engaged a mental health and addiction counselor to meet with him weekly while he gradually tapered his painkiller use. He had been abstinent for 3 years at the time of Fletcher's interview. In addition, he had quit his heavy cigarette smoking and cut his marijuana use by an estimated 80%.[179] It was his personal motivation and commitment that made these results possible. He refused to believe he was not helpless or powerless and so he was not discouraged from working through his own problem.

While, again, the function of counselors in the System's program is not to treat addiction, it is a feature of their role to coach responsible, moderate, drug use. The helpful aspects of the AA and NA teachings can be employed in that coaching effort. Stress is a prime reason to reach for a drug, but here the program removes all the stresses incident to getting drugs. The drugs are too cheap to motivate stealing for the money to buy them, and delivery on time is always assured. Clients are freed also of many environmental cues as they no longer need a drug dealer, no longer devote time to thinking about how to pay for their drugs. Concern for being arrested and jailed is gone. Stabilization can occur here just as we see in medically assisted treatment. The addict can focus more attention on incentives of healthy living, and move however gradually in that direction.

The likelihood of success is increased by several factors including the improvement of life-style and living conditions. Fletcher observes that people able to overcome addiction generally have more "recovery capital."[180] Recovery capital includes having good health and financial assets, safe and sober housing, education and vocational skills, abilities to solve problems, self-esteem, a sense of meaning and purpose, social skills, supportive relationships and healthy leisure activities. If you have some, or all, of these things going for you, it's logical you will find it easier to get sober. The System counselors cannot supply all these, but will certainly supply many of them and help their addicted clients to acquire others.

There is also the potential in the new System to address the addict's isolation. Addiction is usually, if not always, associated with a feeling of being unwanted in society. The person withdraws from the very social interaction they need. One who is not yet addicted, but thinks she is different from others and lacking in respect is a prime candidate for addiction. The drug substitutes for a social life by instilling a sense of well-being. missing in one who feels no one cares. Heroin addicts have said the first hit felt like a huge, warm hug. If that's what you need, why wouldn't you go back for more?

Learning responsible use will be hard for many. To help clients along on that, the counselors can coach in them ways to avoid cues just as 12-Step groups do. Also, as I discuss elsewhere, experienced probation officers are good candidates to serve as counselors. They are well acquainted with cognitive behavioral therapy. And, the social need piece supplied in 12-Step groups, might be supplied with groups organized by the counselors, not in the AA model, but as discussion groups aimed at learning from each other what helps to make responsible use easier.

Positive incentives can also be supplied in the new System. Research experiments show the value of competitive games in developing incentives to change habits. Features of human nature include that we are keen on games of chance and friendly competition. In Bangalore, India, 14,000 morning commuters were given credit points if they clocked into work before 8:30 a. m. at the Infosys plant. Earned credits were like lottery tickets for cash prizes. Soon the number of workers arriving before 8:30 doubled and rush hour traffic congestion dropped.

Another experiment proved the point about friendly competition. To encourage employees to walk more for better health, a company equipped three thousand employees with pedometers to record electronically the number of steps they took each day. Points were earned and used to play a game called Chutes & Ladders, a two-person board game. Cash awards could be won. The game was a hit. Walking began to increase. A friends list and online news feed was added so friends could compare their success, and walking increased even more. Steps per employee per day increased an average of 664, more than a quarter mile. These and other trials of the theory continue to show success in motivating human behavior.[181]

How could the System use these ideas? Such games could be set up by the program operator or in the community by service clubs such as the Lions, Soroptimist, Rotary, Junior League, the Elks, or by a charitable organization such as the Salvation Army or other non-profit public benefit organizations. While many clients of the program would want to retain confidentiality, some will be willing to participate in small groups so long as their identities are not made public. Privacy and confidentiality could also be maintained with code names or numbers. Points could be awarded for each one percent reduction in their drug purchases over, say, a six-month period. The work of scientists such as Hart, show that small incentives can have substantial effect. The lottery/competition work of Stanford University computer scientist Balaji Prabhakar shows that having fun and winning prizes are strong motivators for behavior changes.[182]

It should be apparent from these discussions that, without offering rehab, the program certainly does encourage use reduction and progress in self-development of the kind that leads to addiction recovery.

Moreover, the information rich counseling assures clients are well informed on the science of treatment and the rehab programs available to any client expressing interest in taking that direction.

The System recognizes that immediate abstinence is often not a realistic goal. The drug court's insistence on immediate abstinence may actually work against progress toward eventual recovery by one not yet ready to commit to the work. It induces stress that in some works to send them into Korb's "downward spiral" making the work of recovery more difficult. It follows, as night follows day that drug addicts have a better chance of finding their way if they are supplied with helpful information, encouraged by a friendly coach, and aided in building a better self-awareness. Allowed to continue using, but responsibly, while maturing toward the moment when the addict is ready to quit, helps bring on that moment sooner. Forced abstinence just adds to the load of stress and more guilt when relapse occurs. It takes time for the young and addicted to discover their own abilities and to learn they are responsible for doing the work of getting well. The System I propose provides that learning.

The System promotes recovery also in providing information to its clients from the medical field. Clients having trouble moderating their use to responsible levels might be interested in moving to medically assisted treatment (MAT) and counselors would be equipped to help them access that.

Volkow, et. al. note: "Medications are among the most effective interventions for substance use disorders for which they are available. (Nicotine, alcohol and opiates)."[183]

In a number of countries, heroin is itself now used in treating recalcitrant addicts. These "HAT" clinics opened in Switzerland in 1994 as part of a three-year trial to see if their huge HIV problem might be helped. The reduction in opioid related deaths and HIV infections was immediate. In 1997, the government expanded the program, specifically targeting the long-term users who had not succeeded with other treatments. Patients come into the clinic twice a day for consumption of the drug under supervision. Health outcomes have improved significantly; heroin dosages have stabilized, usually in two or three months, rather than increasing as some had feared; illicit heroin (and illicit cocaine) consumption is significantly reduced; a large reduction in acquisitive crime among participants occurred; heroin from the trials was not diverted to illicit markets; initiation of new heroin use fell; and patients seeking treatments other than HAT, especially methadone, increased.[184]

What we see with MAT is the opposite of what skeptics say of use toleration. It does not inevitably enable addiction, promote increased use, or lead to crime and violence, but a reduction in social ills. Some doctors in the U.S. are now allowed to practice limited heroin based therapy.

So far, medically assisted treatment, MAT, is used mainly to help with opioid and cocaine dependence. However, encouraging research is in progress on a drug to relieve methamphetamine craving.[185]

Tolerating the use of a drug that relieves psychic pain gives patients the time and space they need to find their individual way to getting better. The System's program of dispensing drugs is obviously not the same as MAT or HAT, but it has the potential to work in similar fashion. Moreover, some clients will likely be willing to switch from drugs such as heroin to methadone or buprenorphine and live more productive lives than before.

Medical science is also showing something else the counselors would teach their clients in their responsible use training. This is the importance of nutrition, exercise and sleep. According to MedlinePlus, a service of the U.S. National Library of Health,[186] the following tips help in addiction recovery: eat nutritious meals and snacks; get physical activity and enough rest; reduce caffeine and stop smoking, if possible; seek help from counselors or support groups on a regular basis; take vitamin and mineral supplements.

The System does not "enable" addiction

Here counselors teach and insist upon responsible use, a behavior change and the first step on the way to recovery.

Addicts do not want to be addicts, but motivation to quit may take time to develop. Here is how Satel and Lilienfeld describe it:

> In the early phase of addiction, drugs or alcohol become
> ever more appealing, while once-rewarding activities,
> such as relationships, work, or family, decline in value.
> The attraction of the drug starts to fade as consequences
> accrue –spending too much money, disappointing loved

ones, attracting suspicion at work – but the drug still retains its allure because it blurs psychic pain, suppresses withdrawal symptoms and douses intense craving. Addicts find themselves torn between the reasons to use and the reasons not to.[187]

Counselors in the program can help their addicted clients through these stages with information and encouragement–suggesting incentives and methods that have worked for others.

A depressed, demoralized person who sees little opportunity for a better life, will take longer to discover an incentive to quit drug use than otherwise. Examples include an imprisoned mother, who has lost custody of her child, an unemployed person with a prison record and diminished employment opportunities, and a person with limited coping skills who can't seem to get anything right. Then there are people whose social life is so bound up in using drugs with their friends they cannot imagine happiness without drugs.

We need to confront this question: which approach is more likely to produce addiction recovery: patience with continued drug use accompanied by counseling and encouragement to be more productive and optimistic? Or demanding abstinence, with threats of jail, which can only stigmatize and isolate the person further from friends, family and others? Most of us know that a positive outlook makes it easier to work on self-improvement—feeling stressed, stigmatized and depressed only makes it harder.

Bear in mind, also, that a probable 90% of those who start using illegal drugs do not become addicted to them.[188] And most who do, eventually quit on their own. The remaining few who need treatment will, for the most part, eventually succeed in improving their behavior if they are adequately motivated and stick with it. Counselors help with that.[189]

The System is no more "enabling" in the usual sense of that word than medically assisted addiction treatment. Both work to bring about stabilization. Additional counseling fosters moderated use for however long it takes for the individuals to come to their senses, helping them get there sooner.

Chapter 8:

The System in Focus: a Dynamic Program

It is one of the happy incidents of the federal system that a single courageous State may, if its citizens choose, serve as a laboratory; and try novel social and economic experiments without risk to the rest of the country.

Justice Louis Brandeis

Let's now bring into sharper focus the framework of the new System's program of dispensing drugs–maintaining controls with its rules and the coaching and monitoring of its clients.

Until the Supreme Court rules otherwise, the gestation of our System can only begin at the level of the U.S. government, with a law allowing the States to experiment with customized versions of it. Each State should be allowed to choose its form of operating entity. Subject to federal guidelines, each State would also choose which drugs would be included, staffing requirements, and the regulations it deems appropriate to govern the program. This accords with the recommendations of the Report of the Global Commission on Drug Policy, which, among other things, recommends policies that: "Encourage experimentation by governments with models of legal regulation of drugs to undermine the power of organized crime and safeguard the health and security of their citizens."

To appreciate the importance of each element of the System, let's keep the following objectives in clear focus:

Making drugs unavailable to minors. This first objective aims to protect them from impairing their education and career chances, as well as from addiction. As mentioned before, this is the age at which 90% of addiction starts.

Crime reduction and public safety. A new system should aim to destroy the illicit drug trade—ending the risks of adulterated and toxic substances, along with the crime and violence associated with trafficking.

Promotion of public health. A new system should include features to reduce the risk of falling into substance use disorders and to help those already afflicted to resolve their disorders as efficiently as they can.

Fiscal efficiency. A new system should offer the optimum ratio of costs to benefits in treatment and prevention of substance disorders to ease the burdens on our local, state and national economies.

And so. we turn to the essential details.

DISPENSARY OPERATIONS

Once a client of the System has been qualified and his or her drug type, dosages, delivery locations and agreed supply intervals have been established, the dispensary can then receive and fill the person's orders and deliver them. Once set up, delivery is direct from the warehouse, though under the watchful eye of the counselors on whose computer screens any discrepancy or deviation in orders would pop up. Clients must place their order for each up-coming supply interval. This is to avoid automatic delivery to a client who has decided to abstain for a time or permanently. There would be no delivery without a specific order consistent with the client's plan or use protocol. There would be no direct or personal access to the dispensary. Orders would be done by telephone, fax, email or online.

DRUG DELIVERY

In most cases delivery will be to the client's home by U.S. Mail, private transport companies, or direct delivery by program personnel. To assure that drug deliveries are not high-jacked, diverted or pilfered enroute, an assessment is made at the outset by the counselor and an agreement reached with the client as to the most suitable methods, locations and times of delivery. In neighborhoods and multi-family dwellings where there is a risk of interference by others the client may be required to pick up his delivery at a different location, such as a drop off station maintained by the dispensary, a treatment center, the counselor's office or a consumption site. By the year 2022, some users might climb aboard a robocar and ride to wherever the drop point or consumption site happens to be.

As with any other business, it is essential to the success of the System that its customers' needs be accommodated—especially where the risk of withdrawal symptoms loom. Street dealers will exist for as long as they think they can out-compete the legal System. To remove any inclination to buy from illegal dealers, clients are assured that their orders will be delivered without delay. The dispensary computer system could help to assure this. Special situations, such as when a client has binged and run out of his ordinary supply ahead of schedule, the counselor can step in to help with an interim supply—along with a serious talk about the consequences of such rule breaking.

FACILITIES

The physical facilities will include the administrative and counselor staff offices, plus a warehouse and delivery building.

For security and economic reasons, the inventory of drugs will likely be maintained in remote locations, well away from the counselor offices. In time, it is foreseeable that large-scale dispensaries would serve multiple programs. It is conceivable also that links directly to the pharmaceutical companies could be set up and distribution go out directly from them. The counselor staff facilities are likely to be typical office layouts centrally located. In some areas, such as major cities, it might be feasible to have several smaller satellite offices widely dispersed to place counselors closer to their clients.

LEGAL ENTITY

The legal entity or form of the organization that operates the program will vary. In Chapter 9 three different entity forms are discussed along with the advantages and disadvantages of each. In all cases, however, the operating entity is licensed and regulated to assure adherence to specific State legal standards. The entity will in all cases be a well-funded company of sufficient size, resources and qualified personnel it can be trusted to operate with integrity and sound business practices.

NEW CLIENT INTAKE

Each state may impose different qualifying requirements and criteria for incoming clients. At minimum, these would include detailed interviews with trained counselors to make sure the person applying to the program is in fact an adult, and mentally able to obey the rules at least minimally. Some states might restrict participation to persons who are habitual users or addicts while other states might open the program to all comers. It seems likely the states would offer the service only to those believed to be regular users. The qualifying standards should be sufficiently liberal to maximize participation by users who otherwise patronize the illegal trade. Even unreliable people can be encouraged to correct their behavior over time—meanwhile withdrawing their business from the illegal trade.

The counselors would employ various techniques to evaluate each prospective client and to decide upon an appropriate schedule and frequency of visits, frequency of blood or urine sampling, any special accommodations or security provisions needed. These might include, questioning the applicant, reviewing referral letters of the drug court or other professionals, cognitive ability testing, physical and mental examinations, and speaking with friends and family members as the counselor might think necessary. Some who show a high level of stability and responsibility will not require counselor visits more often than, say, twice per year, whereas others will be deemed to need monthly or even bi-weekly visits.

Special considerations would include the protection of children in the home and other sensitive situations. A prospective client who is pregnant and addicted to heroin would be required to begin immediately a regime of methadone or buprenorphine treatment for the duration of her pregnancy. Ideally each operating entity would employ a physician, able on short notice to examine and provide advice to any new client exhibiting a special health issue.

CLIENT CONTRACT

To qualify as a client of the program each applicant must, execute a written contract spelling out a commitment to responsible use and detailing the various rules to be followed as part of that commitment. These deal with such topics as required random blood or urine testing at the counselor's discretion (medical device technology is progressing at a rapid pace and new devices may replace or render these forms of testing obsolete); counselor visits, at agreed locations and times; cooperation in receiving and demonstrating understanding of pertinent drug information, and the need to keep the drugs safely secured against use by others, especially children; and a commitment to refrain from impaired driving or using around hazardous machinery. Each state will detail the rules it requires. The counselor will refer the clients to their written contract, whenever it becomes necessary to remind them of their commitments, or to threaten expulsion from the program for irresponsible use. The contract would also make clear the consequences of cheating, for example, by buying illegal drugs as well as those dispensed. These consequences include more frequent blood or urine sampling, restrictions as to place and/or time of use, possible referral to drug court, and ultimately being dropped from the program.

CLIENT PAYMENTS

Clients make their payment arrangements at the beginning and these are spelled out in the contract. These will include credit or debit card authorizations, periodic advance payments, online payment, as with Pay Pal, and automatic bank transfers, as well as mailed in cash or a check. Clients without adequate resources to pay for their drugs will not be turned away. These must be accommodated either at no charge, or with deferred charges secured by a lien on property owned or later acquired—just the way state welfare assistance programs work.

Skeptics grimace. Free drugs? Really? Yes, we need to keep our eyes on the prize. We succeed here to the extent we destroy the black market and end the need for destitute addicts to commit crime to buy drugs. All clients must put in their orders for the next interval supply, but they will not be forced to go without safe drugs for lack of money to buy them.

DATA MANAGEMENT

By means of the latest information technology and data management software each client would be identified, tracked, supplied and monitored as to the amount and frequency of use. This information is available to the counselors and used by them to assist in their client monitoring to identify problem cases, and to work more effectively in counseling their clients. Random blood or urine testing to detect blood drug levels that differ from the client's protocol, raising suspicions of cheating, are also recorded in the database for the counselors' information. Differing state and local policies might mandate such testing for all clients for some period, which would serve to clarify the client's level of reliability to follow the rules. Other states might limit testing to certain cases in the discretion of the counselors. Clients found to have broken the commitments of their contracts might be subjected to more frequent meetings and random testing. Reports from the counselors would serve to augment the database on each user so that abuses, such as extra or excessive use, or law violations, or any exposure to a child of drug use or drug access, would be addressed promptly. Risks of referral to drug court and the potential of being dropped from the program should provide strong incentives to follow the rules.

The database could eventually incorporate information from the Prescription Drug Monitoring Programs (PDMPs), operating now in all 50 states. Under these PDMPs, authorized treating professionals access the database as they consider issuing drug prescriptions to their patients. The professional submits a registration form identifying his status and qualifications as physician or counselor of the patient. Once registered the professional can track and check for drug purchase information about the patient instantly to facilitate diagnosis. In our new System access could be allowed to the counselors, to check on clients, not only to the intra-state database, but a database maintained nationwide.

COUNSELORS

Each state would determine the qualifications of the counselors, but at minimum they would need to have some college, or educational equivalent and demonstrate experience or skillsets of a reasonably high order. These professionals will need to command the respect as well as the goodwill of their clients. They will be more effective if thought of by their clients as kindly coaches, who are there to help them with ordinary life challenges and to learn to use responsibly without coercing them toward unwanted rehab. Experienced probation officers will make excellent System counselors. They would need to switch their orientation from law enforcement to the counseling relationship here. But, they are typically well versed in cognitive behavioral therapy the techniques of which will be useful in responsible use training.

Once the System becomes widespread and the need for many thousands of counselors emerges, we should expect colleges to offer full counselor training curricula. Until then the operating entities will need to provide or arrange for the special training necessary. New hires will often have education in fields such as psychology, drug treatment, nursing and other kinds of counseling. However, the counselor position is not one requiring the kind of extensive knowledge one usually expects of a treating professional. Counselors do not treat, they help to educate and encourage their clients, in much the way a trusted friend might do. A graduate in accounting or engineering with good social skills and learning abilities could as well be trained to the job as a clinical psychologist.

The counselors' work involves not only meeting with clients, but keeping up to date on the science of drugs and their effects and implications for users. The counselors must know or have quick access to information on treatment methods and options open to clients who show interest in quitting. In the role of coach and friend to each client, the counselor will also spend time helping on issues of daily living such as jobs, housing and even for some, clothing and food supply. In addition, counselors will undoubtedly interface with city and county officials, school districts and law enforcement from time to time. They need to be articulate, patient, and understanding.

When clients show interest in rehab, the counselors can provide literature and discussions to:

- give the clients a realistic picture of what goes on in residential or outpatient rehab.

- uncover misunderstandings of clients about the nature of addiction and treatment and dispel them.
- provide information about distinct types of treatment and ways to recover.
- Help them to find quality treatment as may be requested.

The counselors work with their clients in other ways as well. Follow-up visits are carried out to keep information about each client up-to-date. Monitoring, including random blood or urine testing enables the counselors to spot problem situations such as addicts at risk for overdosing or law breaking. As noted above, clients caught breaking the rules would be subject to consequences appropriate to the seriousness of the violation.

Each counselor would be assigned a caseload of clients within his or her ability to give all the time required for monitoring and counseling. As previously noted, where the state requires marijuana to be in the System, most clients there would be pot smokers who would not usually require intensive monitoring. A counselor with a high proportion of pot smokers could handle more clients than one with a high proportion of hard drug users. The counselor might need only to conduct a follow up interview with a pot smoker on a semi-annual basis, with very little blood or urine testing. Likewise, clients using heroin, cocaine or meth, but only in amounts suggesting only occasional or responsible use, might be allowed to go with less monitoring than those demanding higher amounts.

Group meetings with willing clients could help to make use of counselor time more efficient, reducing the number of individual visits. These could include discussions among clients about the problems they have encountered and solutions that worked. Encouraging them to offer ideas for ways to improve the system would encourage them to think of the program as in their interests, while stimulating in them a positive self-respect. Moreover, as we saw in Chapter 7, the addicted often benefit from feeling part of a group and the gain of more social life. Clients who participate would benefit and counselors would save time in their monitoring function.

NO COERCION TOWARD REHAB

Some readers may wonder why rehab is not part of the program. A major objective here is to keep drug users in the program and away from street dealers. They should be made to feel comfortable with their counselors and free from any unwanted lecturing or pestering to stop using or to seek treatment. Many clients of the System will not be ready for or interested in discussing treatment and their resolve to follow the rules could be weakened by discontent with the counseling. Most hard-core users would resist joining a program with a reputation for pushing unwanted rehab.

The counselors provide the users with pertinent information on drug science, but do not broach the subject of treatment except upon express or implied invitation by the client. If the client voluntarily speaks about ways toward recovery—and nearly all will in time do so–or specifically requests information along those lines, the counselor is equipped to provide it. But, the counselor's mission is first to be an informative, trusted friend who only gives rehab advice where it is wanted.

This is not rule out a separate rehab clinic offered by the operating entity. Just as safe injection facilities around the world offer rehab as well as clean needles and injection spaces, the program operator could operate a rehab service as well. It is merely important to be clear to all potential clients that the rehab service is separate and they will not be cajoled by their counselors to quit and go to rehab.

CLIENT PRIVACY

Clients would be assured of confidentiality and privacy. It is part of the counselors' job to make necessary accommodations in drug delivery and the times and places of client visits which help to assure privacy protection. Clients are issued photo and genetically coded ID cards to show the police in the event they were stopped for some reason and found to possess their drug. The special ID card would show their standing in the program, and the officer could radio headquarters and have prompt verification of the client's good standing in the program. If the drug in the person's possession were found not to be a legally dispensed one then a drug offense arrest would take place. And, of course, any non-drug offense involved in the stop would still result in arrest.

The confidentiality of registered users would be strictly maintained against government agencies, and the public, with the exception that a client could be subject to referral to drug court for persistent failure to follow the rules.

An exception to user confidentiality would be spelled out in the user's contract in which he would acknowledge that should it become apparent or reasonably suspected that a client with a mental health problem has become a danger to himself or others, the counselor must employ the state legal procedures in taking steps to move the client into some form of emergency care or treatment. This contract clause to this effect might discourage some users from signing and becoming clients of the System, but this should be an infrequent problem we can live with.

Any person who is detained for drug use and who cannot produce a registration card would remain detained until the online search revealed his registration status. Persons not registered clients of the program would be subject to all the same penalties as apply to illegal drug users. Anyone, including registered clients, caught selling drugs meet the same punishment fate as under existing law. Clients might also be subject to suspension from the program, subject to reinstatement after doing jail time or otherwise paying for their offense.

LIABILITY WAIVER

Could clients of the program sue the program operator for damages if they were injured or made ill by the products dispensed? The problem of liability for suit and damages for such claims might be handled in one of two ways. If liability insurance carriers are willing to issue adequate coverage of the operating entity at suitable premiums clients could have a right of action for negligence in its dealings with them. Absent an adequate insurance market for this kind of activity, there would probably need to be some form of legal protection against the potentially numerous claims. Each state would need to enact its own law granting special immunity to the program operators. Without either insurance or immunity—or at least some cap on damages amounts—operating risks might be daunting in some cases.

For a special or enterprise district form of operating entity with taxing authority (see Chapter 9) this liability problem would be no different than that faced by municipal governments.

If the state authorizes immunity contracts, each client of the System could be required to sign a written waiver of all claims or demands upon the operating entity, the counselors and the State, based on injury or illness related to his or her drug use and the dispensation procedures. Each also acknowledges assumption of all risks of using drugs supplied in the program. The law would need to extend immunity to the company, all persons employed by it and the manufacturers of the drugs supplied from all claims or lawsuits by participants based upon health effects of drug use generally or use of the drugs purchased in the System.

Optional functions for the operating entity

By offering related services, the operating entity might increase revenues and its resources to strengthen the program. Some additional services which a System operator might offer either for additional revenue or for community service, include the following.

1. Assisting health officials. Counselor expertise and the data collections and experience acquired in operating the System would hold excellent value for local and state governments. Community

prevention efforts could be well served through cooperation with System personnel with public outreach programs related to prescription drug abuse, for example, and child protection.

2. Operation of community health centers providing addiction treatment services. Such centers might offer psychiatric and psychological treatment in the community, along with addiction treatment. Such a center would work synergistically with the System counselor staff, giving them access to psychologists and medical doctors who can evaluate high-risk clients. Such cases need to be given special attention. For example, a client engaged in conduct dangerous to him or others, or seen as a high-risk for doing so, might be required to have consultations at the community health center as a condition of continuing in the program. A close working relationship between the center and the counselor staff would facilitate the evaluation of problem cases and help in determining special needs of individual users. At the same time, these centers would benefit from the data collection system in spotting patterns and trends.

3. Screening services for the courts. A type of court program with which the counselors in this System might be helpful is one developed for first time DUI arrestees charged with driving under the influence of alcohol levels alleged to be .15% or higher. Because the court deems such arrestees to be high-risk problem drinkers, prompt screening is needed to determine whether they need special handling at the sentencing stage. The availability of experienced counselors could help in this, as well as to provide similar services to the court in drug cases.

4. Subsidizing client treatment. Accumulated surplus revenues from System operations might be sufficient to enable subsidizing of treatment costs and remove this obstacle to a client's getting treatment he might want and need. Surplus revenues might also be invested in affordable housing properties to meet temporary client needs.

5. The System operating entity could offer proprietary marijuana clubs operated somewhat like saloons, where adult marijuana users could socialize with others in comfortable settings, overseen by "bartenders" who would not permit reckless abuse or the using of other drugs in combination with marijuana. A customer

here showing signs of irresponsible drug use would be ushered out. These businesses could provide both revenue to the program operator and tax revenue to the county and state. No product would be allowed to be carried off the premises. Existing clients of the System, in states including cannabis in their program, would have their purchases in the bar entered into the program database for tracking the amount of their consumption.

6. Education programs in the K-12 schools and the colleges and universities by experienced counselors might also be offered. These could be compensated from education budgets.

7. Consumption rooms, also known as supervised injection sites, could be maintained. These operations, staffed by nurses, such as the Insite facility in Vancouver, discussed in Chapter 3, show value in promoting responsible use. In our use tolerant system, they would serve as facilities where both program clients, and those users of injectable drugs, would have a private, clean place to use, with a nurse present and able to help in cases of accidental overdose. This idea, currently helping to prevent HIV and overdose is catching on in the U.S. Several cities are seeking federal authorization to allow them. The Insite experience has been especially positive in saving lives from overdose.

I have not tried here to imagine all operational aspects of the program. State legislatures and regulators will provide the framework and each program operator will work out the details of operation. Each State will make its own judgments and each program will learn through experience how the program functions best and will also observe and copy-cat methods that worked in other locales. As pilot programs show promise in the communities where operated, other counties or states will be attracted toward acceptance of the idea. Interest will be especially enhanced in other locales when dealers move into them seeking business lost in those where the System is working. Savings from reductions in law enforcement expenses (police, courts, jails and prisons) will be envied in other jurisdictions.

Some users will be reluctant to participate for assorted reasons. In time, however, based on what we know of human nature it is likely the reluctant ones will come around, attracted by the low cost, safer legal drugs, a supply as regular and reliable as with prescription drugs, and the avoidance of arrest and punishment.

Nor should we conclude that illicit drug trafficking will immediately cease upon implementation of the Plan. Gangsters and die-hard dealers will continue to try to profit from drugs and some users will continue to patronize them. But the revenue flow away from the criminals will certainly be enormous and will certainly reduce the viability and profitability of their business. As we noted above, this was the conclusion of the Global Commission on Drug Policy. Progress will take the form of increasing numbers of neighborhoods and whole communities becoming just too unprofitable for dealers to do business there—concentrating them in ever smaller spaces where law enforcement can focus resources. We have seen this dynamic at work in neighborhoods where residents have actively opposed drug use and dealing. The absence of profitable business drove them away.[190]As the idea spreads within the U.S. and on to other countries the crime cartels and gangs will suffer heavy blows to their resources. Some will content themselves with other forms of crime, but some will disband. As their revenues decline and their resources weaken, they will be less able to resist law enforcement actions to roll them up.

Is this a "rosie scenario?" Yes, but one based on realistic assumptions. The proof will come as pilot programs are set up and gather experience.

Chapter 9:

The Operating Organization

Bureaucracy kills people's ability to try new ideas.

Walter O'Brien

It is hard to imagine a more stupid or more dangerous way of making decisions than by putting those decisions in the hands of people who pay no price for being wrong.

Thomas Sowell

The legal form

The happy picture, with which we began Chapter 1, will take time to emerge as the states begin to experiment with pilot programs and tentative steps in adopting the System. Choosing the right form of organization will be highly important. Some states may try to initiate the system as a function of a state agency, though I hope not. As the Sowell quote suggests, it would be a mistake to think that an agency of government could successfully develop and operate such a demanding business. Each operating organization will require people with skills and motivations needed to tailor a business plan for the community or region assigned to it. Experienced managers will be needed to carry out the plan and revise it as emerging needs may dictate. Hiring and managing the operations staff will require business oriented people with specialized skills. Capital formation will require financial and banking expertise. Government bureaucracies are not the folks one first thinks of for the stand-up and operation of a successful business—they are people who "pay no price for being wrong."

Politicians who reflexively seek government expansion and regulatory control can be expected to decry the horrors of an operation running under private enterprise principles. How, they will ask, could we expect a business operator not to advertise, promote and encourage drug use? One prominent writer has even suggested that such an entity, given monopoly status over a territory, would be invested necessarily in creating more addicts with whom to do business. These concerns may suggest strong reasons to adopt the enterprise district form or organization discussed below. Ordinary business principles are important to avoid the kind of waste and corruption that can occur in an agency through which large sums of money pass to be handled without the discipline of the "bottom line," or in the case of non-profits and enterprise districts, accountability to constituents. The word corporation is held in low esteem, by many, but here we are speaking of an organization licensed by the State to carry out a specified state regulated mission. We do not need to fear profit-making run amok—especially as today we have high tech means of gathering data and using it to evaluate operations.

Running the entity like a business helps assure taxpayers against waste. Though as I show below a for-profit corporation is not my first choice for the operating organization, it could work without fear of run-away greed. There is no reason to think that an organization properly chartered under suitable regulations cannot be trusted to follow the rules which, among other things, would outlaw any attempt to promote drug use or addiction. The training of the counselors who should come from the fields of psychology, health care, sociology and law enforcement among others should produce a cadre of professionals who will take pride in what they are doing. We don't fear that dentists are promoting poor dentition to increase clientele. We don't find our utility companies encouraging us to waste electricity or gas? Most business merchants are motivated to sell you on the need for their products, but we would be surprised to hear a lawyer urging his client to commit crime to create more defense business. Professional pride is a strong motivator of professional conduct, especially when it is backed up by insistent regulation.

In exchange for territorial monopoly the state would exact a commitment to acceptable practices and cooperation with regulatory oversight. Just as banks are subject to audits by the government, and utilities monopolies are required to share some decision making with a government commission, so too would we expect a company dispensing mind altering drugs to be under the close scrutiny of regulators.

The choices of organization form include three: a for-profit corporation, a non-profit corporation, or an entity known as a special district, or enterprise district. The legal form of the entity is less important than the terms under which it is chartered, staffed and regulated. For reasons, I will discuss further on, I think the special district is the best format for this kind of operation, but I will briefly discuss the three choices mentioned in order.

1. A for-profit corporation is an organization vested with rights to operate a legal enterprise, through the agency of its directors and officers. Just like a natural person, if it breaks rules and contracts it can be sued in court and found liable for damages, or ordered to do or refrain from doing things to the injury of others. Criminal charges can be brought against a corporation and penalties imposed upon it as well as upon any of its officers for wrongdoing. For-profit corporations are in effect owned by their shareholders who provide the investment capital enabling it to buy, lease or build its facilities, purchase supplies and equipment and

hire its employees. As operations proceed and revenues exceed expenses, the shareholders expect compensation in the form of dividends or rising share certificate values. The officers run the business under the supervision of the board of directors who hire them. The law treats directors like trustees who have strictly enforced duties to act in the interests of the company and not put their own personal interests ahead of its. Officers include the president, one or more vice presidents, CEO, treasurer or controller, and secretary, all of whom serve at the pleasure of the board. In turn, the board members are elected by the shareholders and they too can be turned out by shareholder action for inadequate performance. For-profit corporations can be placed under the regulatory control of the State, just as many public utilities are.

2. A non-profit corporation differs in that it does not have investor/owners called shareholders. It does have a board of directors and is operated by officers appointed by the board and salaried, but there is no accountability to an ownership group. The non-profit owns itself and relies on its board to govern it properly. Some non-profit organizations are set up to have members who elect the board of directors. In that arrangement, there is a measure of control by the larger group—the members, but that control is seldom exercised since members gain little or nothing from taking an active interest in management. Members may pay annual dues, which cover little more than meeting expenses, newsletters and perks. Funding of the non-profit's operations typically comes from charitable foundations and private party contributions. However, a city interested in encouraging a controlled dispensary operation can help fund it from the city treasury.

Non-profits are set up either for the mutual benefit of their members or to carry out some public purpose such as a religious, educational or charitable project. These entities are usually accountable to the State for following regulatory guidelines and proper management of their funding, and they are subject to auditing by the state. Like any other corporation they can exist only by the issuance of articles of incorporation, a form of charter, by the State. Under the federal and state tax laws public benefit non-profits may be given tax exemption status making them income tax-free and contributions to them tax deductible.

3. A special district sometimes called an "enterprise district" when it operates a business and a "municipal tax district" when allowed to raise revenues through property taxes, would be an excellent fit for a controlled dispensary operation. Capital needs are often raised by districts through bond measures approved by the voters and backed up by district revenues. Bonds are the contracts by which they borrow money from investors. Special districts are considered political subdivisions. Within the specified area of their purposes, they operate separately from either the agencies of state government or the county and city governments. Still they are usually under the thumb of a regulatory state agency. Like corporations they are chartered by the State, required to meet specified qualifications, and operated by officers appointed and overseen by a board of directors. The governing board is elected by the voters in the district territory, so the directors are accountable to them as well as the state for proper management of their assets and business. The reader may know of such an entity operating as a water company or a sewage district or other utilitiy provider.

As each state legislature considers implementation of a controlled drug dispensary program, it will decide which of these entity types will best serve its purpose. Each offers certain attributes which may offer an advantage depending upon the community it serves. If for example, in a given area the judgment is that profit making would be difficult because of the scarcity of users in a low-density region, the special district with taxing authority might serve best. Revenues from drug sales would be augmented by tax collections. In a major city, however, the business plan based on long term stable drug sales might be chosen, raising capital from the private investors rather than through taxation. Where a service area has a high proportion of problem drug users, many more counselors might be needed than in one where most drug use is typically more moderate. The employment of the non-profit corporation form would more likely be considered where it can depend for its funding on grants and charitable donations or payment from the city. Many foundations, such as the well-known Bill and Melinda Gates Foundation, are looking for worthy projects to place their money. Such foundations can provide ongoing funding to supplement drug sale income and remove the need for both private capital or taxpayer support. The entity formation choice is a question of policy and economics, which we need not resolve here.

The special district form has some especially attractive features.

Besides being more appealing to those with an anti-corporation view, there are some advantages offered by the special district, because it can be set up with taxing authority and a board of directors elected by the residents of the district area it serves. As previously noted a district is responsible to the people who reside within its territory. And given taxing authority it will be scrutinized, you can be sure, by the local people among whom the board members and officers will live and work. Just as a local school district board must satisfy its constituents and be elected by them, so too would a regional narcotics district. Moreover, in each city or town there is a community health officer whose job is to keep an eye out for health issues which affect community health. Typically, these officials are concerned with disease vectors such as insects, rodents and dirty needles, water and food supply safety, and health related epidemics. A health official would logically be expected to work in coordination with the local System operator and publicly criticize any inadequate or untoward activities or deviations from mandated procedures.

Tax revenues will likely need to supplement drug sales, because of the high costs of the counselor program. Yikes, who wants more taxes? Nobody does. Yet, a well-funded program can be effective in regulating drug user conduct, At the same time the drug dispensation program drives the criminal traffickers off to seek greener pastures elsewhere. The overall effect of that will be savings in law enforcement and health care costs and the lowering of taxes, not raising them. Lower emergency room visits and doctor bills help reduce health care costs and insurance rates. We have already discussed the benefits of removing drug dealer accessibility to minors and the crime reduction savings to be realized by law enforcement, the justice system, and so forth. Health care costs will reflect less waste in rehab treatment failures. Reductions in city, county and state expenses related to drug law enforcement and addiction treatment will offset and likely exceed any small property tax increases. A county-wide district that has, say, 500,000 residential, commercial and industrial properties with an average valuation of \$250,00 on each, a mere two one-hundredths of one per cent, (about \$50), assessment would raise \$25 million per year. The tax burden would be small, yet what a boon to the community in enforcement and community health savings.

Thinking about revenues and losses in a System operation

Because there will be so many variables affecting cost of operation from place to place, we cannot reasonably estimate how well a given System operator might cover expense of the program with drug sales. How much in tax revenues might be needed for an individual program would depend upon two main variables: 1) the overall costs as determined by the size of the administrative and counseling staffs, facilities costs and other overhead expenses, and 2) the volume of drug sale revenues available to it.

In a program with 60,000 users and potential clients, including marijuana users, about one-third would be hard drug users. In states where marijuana has been legalized and so is not included, the client count would be reduced by about 2/3rds to 20,000. Demographic studies of an area will determine the ratio of the use of one drug type in relation to the others. Demographics also will determine how many impecunious clients must be given the drugs without up-front payment or any payment at all. These variables and many more must inform any business plan and the business analysis to be made.

Still it is useful to note that with a clientele of 20,000, it would take only per-client monthly sales of $100 to realize an annual gross revenue of $24 million; or with a clientele of 60,000, a gross revenue of $72 million. Most drug users spend more than that. Only if drug sale revenues and/or charitable contributions are insufficient to cover costs, will it be necessary to resort to local taxation. However, as mentioned the tax burden should be quite small, especially in relation to the tax savings accruing in the law enforcement and health fields.

What about the ratio of counselors to clients? The size of the counselor staff would account for the largest cost of doing business. That ratio depends upon the mix of drugs being used in the local program. In states where marijuana is legal and not included, the 20,000 clients will likely be served by programs with a higher counselor/client ratio, because supervision of hard drug users means more visits. In states where marijuana is included, counselors with a high proportion of marijuana-only users—or whose clients are mostly responsible, rational users of other drug types, the ratio will be lower than where hard drug usage is a greater part of the mix. We're in the realm of guesswork here, but counselors whose client mix is weighted more toward cannabis users and responsible users would probably be able to serve a clientele of anywhere from several hundred to perhaps more than a thousand. In such situations, the frequency of contact for the most clients would be low – perhaps 2 to 6 times per year. This ratio of client to counselor would drop when the mix contains more problematic users, because more frequent visits would be needed.

In our 60,000-user community, (marijuana included) we might have 20 to 40 counselors for the 40,000 group who use only marijuana or use harder drugs moderately. That means a ratio of one to two thousand clients per counselor with perhaps only two visits per year. For the rest of the clientele the ratio might drop to one counselor per 200 clients and visit frequency might increase to an average of 12 times per year with each counselor conducting 9 or 10 client visits per day. Some of these may be accomplished with group meetings as discussed above. The counselors would need time not only to see clients, but to study scientific updates and to stay abreast of treatment methods and availability, among other things. And so, we add 100 more counselors giving us a total counselor staff of up to 140. A counselor staff of 140 would likely cost $100,000 per year each or $14 million annually, including salary, benefits and payroll taxes. This would be the greatest cost, but probably equaled by all the other expenses bringing the total cost of doing business to about $28 million. Drug sales might cover these, but in many operations, it seems likely that some tax subsidies or charitable contribution will be needed.

While I intend here nothing more than to suggest the general magnitude of costs for a local program, it is apparent such costs are not beyond the realm of the feasible.

Chapter 10:

Benefits to Community Health and Safety

It is time to end the discrimination against people who need treatment for chemical addiction. It is time for Congress to deal with our Nation's number one public health problem.

Former Congressman (R) James Ramstad

Better health in our communities.

Among the unintended consequence of drug use prohibition is that in various ways it works against public health. It degrades our ability to reduce the spread of diseases transmitted with dirty needles and the selling of sex to buy drugs and it maintains an underworld drug trade distributing products often tainted with unsafe additives. The pain medication fentanyl, for example, has been used as a power booster and killed many thousands. In our controlled dispensary System only safely manufactured and chemically pure drugs and paraphernalia are used, eliminating the need addicts sometimes encounter to exchange dirty needles in haste for a hit as withdrawal draws nigh.

Harmful drug additives increase health care concerns and the costs of our health care system. Ecstasy is a drug highly popular among young adults. It is called the "party drug." It is easy to get from uncontrolled sources and poses serious health risks because of additives that make it cheaper. Here is a quote from the American Council for Drug Education, Basic Facts:

> One reason Ecstasy can be especially dangerous is the lack of content control. Ingredients are hard to get and manufacturers of the drug often use substitutes, mixing other harmful additives with the already dangerous mix. This practice is so common that "drug test kits" are often sold with the drug so users can test for purity. Because of the uncertainties about the drug sources, pharmacological agents, chemicals used to manufacture them, and possible contaminants, it is difficult to measure the toxicity, consequences and symptoms that might be expected.[191]

Drug users seldom are given any information as to the purity of what they are getting. Even their trusted dealers may have no knowledge of what might have been added along the distribution channel before they bought the product.

Heroin is cheap in part because of the various additives used to "cut" it and the frequent addition of the cheap opioid fentanyl, used to make it more potent. Fentanyl is said to be up to 50 times more potent than morphine and has been a major factor the opioid overdose death epidemic so prominent in today's news. And, as stated by NIDA "In addition to the effects of the drug itself, street heroin often contains toxic contaminants or additives that can clog the blood vessels leading to the lungs, liver, kidneys, or brain, causing permanent damage to vital organs."[192]

The opioid overdose epidemic is well documented in the daily news. Opioids include a variety of pain medications prescribed by doctors. Fentanyl is such a medication, but it is manufactured illegally too. It is pressed into fake pills that look like the real thing, and it is sold in powder form or added to heroin as a booster. And it is deadly. According to the CDC, opioids were involved in 33,091 deaths in 2015, and opioid overdoses have quadrupled since 1999. Fentanyl is an important part of that.[193]

Similarly, methamphetamine which produces a low-cost high and so is popular in poorer neighborhoods and with young people may contain toxic additives. According to PBS Frontline meth's impact on families and communities is much more devastating and it has become the biggest drug problem across the country.[194]

Meth is a particularly pernicious drug because it stimulates brain centers to release a flood of dopamine creating a highly pleasurable euphoria. The young person who keeps going back for more so compromises the wiring of dopamine receptors, the pleasure response weakens to the point that the drug quits giving any pleasure at all. Yet the craving for it continues. Deep depression is then experienced and the user keeps going back for more trying to fight the depression. Nutrition, health and dental issues follow.

The disease vector of unclean needles has presented a major challenge for some communities. According to the website for the U.S. Center for Disease Control[195] in 2015, 6% (2,392) of the 39,513 diagnoses of HIV in the United States were attributed to injection drug use. The implications are stark. Every year thousands use dirty needles, get sick and become disease vectors themselves. HIV/Aids is not the only disease so transmitted. Hepatitis and venereal diseases are spread that way too. In response, needle exchange programs have been rolling out in some of the hardest hit areas, and where injection sites are allowed (none in the U.S. so far) clean needles are available. But, the problem persists in many communities.

The System envisioned here would dispense only pure drugs of labeled strengths, along with paraphernalia free of infectious risks. The counseling feature makes it far more certain that we can identify and treat health problems before they become severe or life threatening. With the monitoring and counseling conducted on a regular basis by program counselors, we would have a much better chance of heading off unhealthy conduct and of dealing effectively with consequences of such conduct when they occur.

And though the System won't end prostitution, it will eliminate the need to offer sex for drugs, further reducing a common disease vector and helping the unfortunates who have deemed it necessary to sell themselves to live a healthier life.

Might some users take advantage of the System and supplement their supplies by ordering online from overseas, or making drugs such as methamphetamine in their own homes? The System's random blood and urine (or medical device) testing help avoid this. The client who would cheat must always fear detection and possible ejection from the program. The benefits of the program are so great their loss would be a logical deterrent. Still it is certain to happen. Some clients of the program will not be trustworthy. Over longer time periods we may find ways to plug all the leaks, but near term our objectives should emphasize meaningful progress. Perfection might be the goal, but as realists we will take satisfactory progress

A healthier community results also from an increase in the number of addicts in treatment. Addicts who come in from the under-world of illegal drugs and participate in the System will have regular contact with counselors and the information they provide. While the counselors do not offer nor demand rehab of their addicted clients, they help them to stabilize their lives and provide helpful information. It has been amply shown that some addicts will succeed in quitting merely by talking with persons trained in providing encouragement and information about the science of addiction. Moreover, as the evidence shows. when the addicted are accorded dignity and respect, they often respond positively with behavior improvements. The counselors provide a friendly presence in the lives of their addicted clients, serving as helpful and healthy role models. By showing them respect the counselors help them improve their self-awareness and their interest in alternative life styles—the usual first steps toward seeking sobriety.

Another important ingredient of community health is information, based upon scientific knowledge. The counselor is in a unique confidential relationship with the users in the community to provide drug risk profiles and safety information. As an example, consider the designer drug called "Bath Salts" sold in convenience stores and pot shops. Uninformed users of this drug have been seriously sickened. This substance contains a *cathinone*-like molecule like that found in the Khat plant native to the horn of Africa, a substance widely used recreationally in both North Africa and the Arabian Peninsula for thousands of years. There the plant materials are chewed to release the pleasure inducing molecule. The medical understanding of the synthetic product is still developing, but users are likely to be highly ignorant as to how dangerous this crystal form concoction can be. One study found that this drug's ingredients are 10 to 50 times more potent than cocaine. Emergency rooms have reported cases of Bath Salt users becoming psychotic, violent and delirious.[196] By bringing drug users into an information rich system, they can be offered safer drugs and counseled as to the dangers of others. Moreover, is there any doubt, but that in a use tolerant system, the pharmaceutical companies would seek profits in new drug inventions, approved by the FDA, to provide safer alternatives to existing drugs?

Learning through experience and data collection

A feature of the System which offers value to the health of the nation is the data collection that proceeds as experience occurs. John Ramsey, a toxicologist at St. George's Medical School in London and an expert on "legal highs" observed that a zero-toleration policy deprives us of the experience by which we might learn how to gauge the various drug effects. [197] The more we can learn through observations of human experience with drugs, the better we can understand which of them and in what doses are truly harmful, or addicting, on the one hand, the extent to which we might learn to reap benefit in their use. One Coloradan's experience with pot is instructive. Fictitiously called "Isaac", he was a troubled and sometimes violent adolescent. He had an arrest record involving multiple offenses by the age of 17. He started smoking pot and he began to change. His fighting tendencies and his arrests ended. He went to college, studied plant physiology, and did graduate work in bio-chemistry. Now he grows and sells pot, mostly to friends. Some may question whether this is any reason to praise Isaac who was in the illicit trade before his state legalized it. At least we can say that (a) he stopped being a persistent law breaker, and that (b) his experience is useful to our study of how cannabis might be used beneficially.[198]

Security in our communities

The System sets up a program which enables society to begin to know, without violating individual confidentiality, where the addicts are, in what numbers, and what they are using and what they are doing. Data so collected is valuable in studying drugs, their use and effects. The data so collected would likely be valuable to scientists and researchers in developing the drug knowledge so vital for users to have. For example, we have scientific information suggesting prolonged marijuana use during the teen years impairs mental development. Drug using parents shown proof positive that allowing their teenage children to use pot can seriously harm them, will naturally decline to do so.

While the program protects the confidentiality of its clients, they would be in regular and frequent contact with their counselors who would represent a first line of defense in the event an addict begins to show signs of potentially dangerous behavior. In such cases more frequent blood or urine testing could be imposed along with increased monitoring and warnings of possible ouster from the program and even institutional restraint. Upon entering the program, the client contractually agrees to responsible drug use and a breach of that contract can disqualify him from continuing in it. Under our present system, the addicted who engage in danger-ous drug taking behaviors, such as shooting up many times per day, have, as a practical matter, no oversight and no harm prevention mechanism in place. Our counseling program can help with that.

As noted by the reports of the Global Commission and the Lancet Commission previously cited, current policy is inflicting more harm than good. It is no argument against the System I propose to say that it will supply drugs to addicts who may, under the influence, do things that threaten a community's security. We have these problems under the existing regime, and as noted earlier there is no data support for any worry that the System would increase it. In some neighborhoods, the citizens are so terrified by the gangs with guns that they would rather pull down the blinds, lock their doors, and try to stay safe in isolation indoors. With the System proposed here the greater likelihood is we will all but eliminate the risks to a community of the violence and corruption that accompanies illegal drug dealing.

The distribution of illicit drugs throughout the United States is in the main attributable to criminal gangs, and most of the criminal gang activity involves the use of weapons. We have thousands of inner city gangs and outlaw motorcycle gangs throughout the United States. Efforts focused on gangs and guns have made a difference in reducing the numbers, but they are still huge. Even in farmland valleys and forested foothill regions gun violence is a by-product of competitive drug trafficking which threatens the safety of the innocent citizens who live there. Scott Anderson's book, *Shadow People* is a remarkable piece of investigative reporting which shows the devastation wreaked in the rural meth market.

In chapter 2 we discussed the murder problems of Chicago and other large cities in the country, where gang activities in drug dealing are rampant. As "*Freakonomics*" economist Steve Levitt explains, only the top leaders of these gangs make good money on drugs. Lower level members make as little as $3.50 an hour selling drugs on the street. By taking the profits out of the drug trade the System envisioned here would make most of the gangs penniless and gang loyalty pointless.[199]

Accomplishing goals of law enforcement through drug profit destruction.

A paper published by the Department of Justice in 1989,[200] and considered in the 2011 Report of the Global Commission on Drug Use,[201] provided a detailed summary of the goals of law enforcement in the matter of illegal drugs, and the obstacles presented to their realization. Among the findings reported was the fact that in communities and neighborhoods that are strongly intolerant of drug dealing, the policing problem is far less than it is in those areas where people have been tolerant of drug dealing or have given up efforts to resist through citizen vigilance and control. The paper reveals a telling fact. In communities and neighborhoods where the use of drugs is at a comparatively low level, the dealers don't operate, because it is not profitable for them to do so.[202] Here is what Moore and Kleiman found:

> In some areas, drug dealers cannot gain a foothold. There are too few users to make dealing profitable and too many vigilant people ready to expose and resist the enterprise. Other parts of a city seem to have yielded to the drug trade. Drug users are plentiful. Drug dealers are an influential social and economic force. Local residents and merchants have lost heart.

Clearly the dealers rationally respond to profit opportunities, just as we would expect them to do. This is clear evidence that the use of market forces to kill the illicit drug trade will do so in the system proposed. As areas of drug trade dry up for dealers, their numbers will shrink and those still in business will be more concentrated in smaller areas, where law enforcement has a better chance to detect, interdict their supplies and arrest them. In time, as these programs spread state to state, we should expect the disappearance of all the small-scale dealers and user/dealers. Ultimately the drug crime and violence will end as the cartels and traffickers give up and disappear.

The goals of police action against drug trafficking listed by Moore and Kleiman are:[203]

1. Reduce the gang violence associated with drug trafficking and prevent the emergence of powerful organized criminal groups.
2. Control the street crimes committed by drug users.

3. Improve the health and economic and social well-being of drug users.
4. Restore the quality of life in urban communities by ending street level drug dealing.
5. Help to prevent children from experimenting with drugs, and
6. Protect the integrity of criminal justice institutions.

Their Justice Department paper shows the ineffectiveness of "expressive law enforcement," the principal strategy employed by police departments. This strategy is one of increasing by factors of two or three each and all a department's activities aimed at increasing arrests as the drug problems worsen. There are several justifications for this approach. It seems to appeal to common sense; it is what police departments know how to do; it will to some extent be effective in bringing trafficking under some control by incapacitation and deterrence; and it sustains and animates a general social norm opposed to drug use.[204] But, multiplying resources committed to the problem has not shown itself successful in gaining control of the problem. And so, police departments keep growing even while failing to bend the curve of worsening drug problems. Indeed, since the above cited paper was published (1989) the world has seen how little law enforcement has been able to control it.[205] As the authors say, it disregards the scale and resilience of the drug markets; fails to establish benchmarks for success and amounts to little more than the "promise of a valiant effort to increase arrests."[206]

Now consider the system of toleration with controls such as I have detailed and see how it might compare in accomplishing the DOJ's list of goals.

1. *Reduce gang violence and organized crime.* The System dries up the drug trade and the gangs and trafficking cartels will wither.
2. *Control the street crimes.* It is among the hard-core users and addicts we find those who commit property crimes to finance their needs. By making drugs available at prices

below the street and free to qualified individuals the motive for these crimes evaporates.

3. *Improve the health and well-being of drug users.* The regular, and for some, frequent interaction between the system clients and their counselors gives them the information they need on developments in drug science, health care options, available treatment options, support groups, employment possibilities, and more. As a friend in the life of the user the counselor is also a valuable role model.

4. *Restore the quality of life in urban communities by ending street level drug dealing.* As noted in No. 1 above, market forces will dry up street level drug dealing.

5. *Help to prevent children from experimenting with drugs.* The principle purpose of the control features of the system proposed is just this goal. In this system children cannot access drugs through the legal channel and illegal dealers become fewer and less accessible. Ever shrinking availability of dealers, increasing pressure by law enforcement on the smaller numbers, rising street prices of drugs all combine to curtail experimentation by minors.

6. *Protect the integrity of the justice system.* Most but not all drug law enforcement officers have resisted the temptations on offer in the drug markets. Respect for law enforcement and the criminal justice system suffer. As the System gradually takes hold and spreads, drug interdiction, seizures, shake down opportunities and bribery decline.

Chapter 11:

Including Marijuana? Maybe.

Penalties against possession of a drug should not be more
damaging to an individual than the use of the drug itself;
and where they are, they should be changed. Nowhere
is this more clear than in the laws against possession of
marijuana in private for personal use....

Jimmy Carter, President

Inclusion in the Plan is a state by state determination

Recreational marijuana, as of this writing, is legal and allowed
with little restriction in eight states and the District of Columbia,
with more certain to follow. California, Massachusetts, Maine,
Alaska and Nevada followed the lead of Colorado, Washington
and Oregon. All but six States in the U.S. allow marijuana for
medical use in some form.[207] Statements made by the recently
elected Trump administration, have thrown into question whether
these State allowances will stand in their present form. Federal
law still considers marijuana a Schedule I drug, just as illegal for

possession and use as heroin. And Attorney General Sessions has said he intends to enforce all laws.

Polling by the Pew Research Center indicates that about 52% of Americans (65% Democrats; 37% Republicans) favor legalizing marijuana.[208] Yet, the future of State legalization measures remains obscure.

Predictably, some states will continue to resist legalizing marijuana for recreational use. In those, as well as the others which now allow it, if the federal government clamps down and enforces its laws, the System I propose offers the best alternative solution for marijuana as well as the other drugs. Some marijuana users might prefer the prices and quality assured by System programs in their states.

We are talking hypothetically here, but whether cannabis containing products are to be included in the controlled dispensation System will necessarily be decided on a state by state basis. There will be many voices raised against any sort of control on the personal use of marijuana. Evidence is mounting that, at least for adults, cannabis is a benign, often beneficial substance. In the face of this growing evidence, subjecting it to the System's controls will not be popular in many states. However, it could make sense for those states continuing to resist legalization.

Marijuana comes in various potency levels owing to different percentage levels of the psychoactive molecules called tetrahydrocannibinoids (THC). Some European countries that have decriminalized marijuana use are considering returning marijuana with THC levels of 15% or more to the hard drug category. Potency levels of marijuana might be used in some states to decide whether to include it in the System or not. Other states might insist on including all marijuana products. As of this writing the THC levels of various cannabis products are highly uncertain. Testing labs employ different methods for determining potency and results may vary by as much as 25%.[209]

If potency levels are difficult to ascertain and if cannabis purveyors cannot certify the THC level of their products, more states will likely reject legalization and insist upon inclusion in the

System. A valuable feature of the System is that experience will allow the development of data based upon observations and user reports so that when cannabis products are dispensed both users and counselors will have better information. This experience related value of adult use toleration has been remarked in a similar context. John Ramsey, a toxicologist at St. George's Medical School in London and an expert on so-called legal highs points out how strict prohibitions placed upon various of the newly minted "designer drugs", some of which may not be harmful, deprives us of the experience by which we might learn how to gauge their effects. It also promotes the invention of more new drugs such as synthetic cannabinoids: "We should perhaps be slightly more sparing with bans in our legislation than we are," he said. "When we ban substances, we spawn another range of untested compounds."[210]

As noted earlier, among the optional services System operators might offer, the idea of proprietary marijuana saloons is a good one. Operated much like liquor bars, they could help in promoting responsible use. I'm betting they will come to be called "Pot Pubs." These establishments would offer only cannabis products to be consumed onsite. Adults could go to pot pubs for solitary relaxation, or to join friends for socializing. No other drug or alcohol would be offered or allowed. These could be run by the System operator as revenue producing enterprises.

Alternatively, the program operator could license such bars or pubs to be run by independent entrepreneurs, overseeing operations and charging an annual license fee. These bars could be open to the adult public as well as to clients of the System program. Program clients are bound to follow program rules on penalty of being ejected from the System, and are committed to periodic counseling. As such they could be allowed to receive special discounts and possibly even the privilege of carrying product off premises. Pot smokers who have not become clients might then see a value in doing so. Each state would be free to design and regulate this form of enterprise to meet the preferences of its citizens.

Marijuana use on the rise among young people

Marijuana is often referred to as a soft drug, but that does not mean it has no deleterious effects. The most recent data show that marijuana is used by 19.1% of 18 to 25-year-olds, about the same as in 2011.[211] As any auto insurance company will tell you this is a group of young adults among whom there is a higher incidence of risky behaviors. However, the greater risks attributable to marijuana for hazardous use and addiction are among the 12 to 17-year-old users. SAMHSA found that in 2014 there were 1.8 million in that age group who had used marijuana in the past month—about 7.4 of them. [212]

Adolescence is a bad time for marijuana use. At minimum, it has a demotivating effect. The teen years are the most important for acquiring knowledge and skills that will serve in both choosing the best career path and succeeding in whatever path is chosen. Some research suggests there are harmful physical effects in prolonged marijuana use, though this is controversial. According to Dr. Mitchell S. Rosenthal, M.D., a child psychiatrist, and founder of Phoenix House, the nation's largest nonprofit substance-abuse treatment and prevention organization:

> Pot smoking puts the user at risk of psychosis, changes in the anatomy of the brain, and damage to the heart and lungs. It retards maturation and impairs learning, memory and judgment—no small matters during the adolescent years…. Unfortunately, the part of the brain that censors dumb and dangerous behavior is last to develop. It doesn't generally come fully on line until the mid-20s, but the pleasure-seeking part of the brain is fully functioning by puberty.[213]

Dr. Rosenthal's claims of risks of psychosis, brain changes, and changes to heart and lung have been rigorously challenged in more recent years, though vulnerability to addiction in adolescence is well established. His has been the official position of the DEA, described in a 45-page document available for many years on the Agency's website. But, on the demand of Americans for Safe Access and other organizations, made under the Information Quality Act the DEA took it down. The Act is aimed at assuring accuracy of information given to the public by government agencies, and so we can infer the DEA no longer is so sure about those claims.

Early fears that marijuana serves as a gateway drug have largely been debunked. Just because young persons use pot now and then does not mean they will go on to harder drugs. However, we cannot ignore the fact that teenagers who habitually cope with stress, anxiety or boredom by getting high on pot are not learning to cope with those adversities the way nature intended. Instead of searching out and developing new interests that make adolescent life fun, or at least more bearable, they come to depend on the chemical answer—and personal coping skills normally leading to a happier life are stunted. This is the true gateway to addiction and other drugs may be added later.

While it is highly debatable whether merely using marijuana will lead the young person to try more potent drugs for a more stimulating high, it is not debatable that under our current prohibition regime, where weed is available from dealers of questionable integrity, young users are at some risk of exposure to undesirable influences.

Opposition in the U.S. to legalizing pot

The data cited above show that more than half of us favor the legalization of marijuana, which of course means that close to half do not favor it. This points to a serious political difficulty in changing the status quo. Legalization nationwide would certainly accomplish one of the goals of the proposed System; that of depriving the gangs and cartels of some of their illicit profits as more people begin to grow their own and the price comes down. Two principal arguments for legalizing pot, is that it will drive the crime ridden and often violent illegal business away, plus it can be taxed by state and local governments to the benefit of the taxpayers. However, legalization in the eight states that have adopted it has meant commercialization, meaning they are sold in retail stores just as alcohol is sold. How has that worked out so far? Not as well as hoped.

Drug policy activist Kevin Sabet argues that tax revenues have been disappointing in Colorado and the pot shops are patronized mainly by AARP members and out of state buyers. In other words, he is saying older people who decline to patronize street dealers and out of state buyers who don't know where to find them, are the only ones who buy the legal products. The legal sellers have trouble competing on price because of the high taxation and so the illegal market continues just as before—making pot available to teens and preteens.[214] In a personal interview with a pot shop operator in Washington, she confirmed to me this was true there and likely true in all states.

In their eagerness to remove the bans on marijuana the activists have sold the people and legislators on the idea of great tax revenues. The tax incentive is alluring for many politicians and not a few of their voters. This idea led directly to commercialization. So enthusiastic were people for legalization on the one hand and a new tax revenue source on the other, little thought was given to the alternative—a controlled dispensary accessible only to registered adults. Now the experience in Colorado, perhaps soon to be seen in the other states as well, is that tax revenues have been a fraction of what was expected. The legal retail sellers cannot compete on price with the illegal dealers because of both the many costs of retailing, and the taxes imposed at all levels of government. And, of course, minors have just as much access to pot as ever before.

States allowing pot for medical use have experienced a different kind of problem. Local ordinances in the various counties are adopted to regulate the growing of "medical marijuana." Such laws restrict the number of plants allowed to be grown or the size of the area allowed to be cultivated. These restrictions affecting an activity that is legal invite scofflaw conduct resulting a need for more law enforcement as people grow more than allowed or outside areas permitted. If all marijuana were dispensed in our controlled program, the System, this additional enforcement cost would be materially reduced. Admittedly, our reform would not likely have much effect on those who are willing to risk running afoul of the law by growing their own. This will be an enforcement problem into the future no matter what policies are adopted because of the ease of growing pot for personal use in locations where detection is difficult.

Chapter 12:

Constitutional Weakness of the Federal Drug Laws and the Value of State Experimentation

We hold these truths to be self-evident, that all men are created equal, and that each is endowed by his creator with the right to life, liberty and the pursuit of happiness.

Adams, Jefferson, and Madison in the Declaration of Independence

It is one of the happy incidents of the federal system that a single courageous state may, if its citizens choose, serve as a laboratory; and try novel social and economic experiments without risk to the rest of the country.

Justice Louis Brandeis

The Separation of Powers

Did you ever wonder why the era called Prohibition early last century, banning alcohol, came about through a constitutional amendment, not just a law adopted by Congress? I know, it's not exactly a top of mind issue, but citizens need to understand how their natural rights to pursue happiness can be taken away from them. Under the Constitution as it was understood early last century, we knew we could not just pass a federal law banning alcohol. We had to go through the long and arduous process of amending that supreme legal document. The 18th Amendment had to be ratified by the states, before it went into effect in 1920, banning the manufacture, sale and transportation of "intoxicating liquors." It took us 13 years to learn the lessons of that mistake and undo Prohibition with another amendment: the 21st, adopted in 1933.

Some might say, well, that was only alcohol, not heroin or cocaine. But, that argument does not hold water. Alcohol is no less a drug than those, and poses far greater problems than they do. So why didn't the government just pass a law? It goes back to the Bill of Rights, our first ten amendments. The tenth of those declares: "The powers not delegated to the United States by the Constitution, nor prohibited by it to the States, are reserved to the States respectively, or to the people." And since, there is nothing about drugs in the Constitution, or for that matter controlling by Congress any other consumable of which it might disapprove sometime in the future, it is natural to ask: how can the U.S. Congress pass a law like the Comprehensive Drug Abuse Prevention and Control Act of 1970, banning all the recreational drugs?

When Congress adopted our first national law aimed at drug control, the 1914 Harrison Act, there was nothing in that law prohibiting the manufacture, sale, possession or transport of drugs. It was designed as a tax law clearly within Congressional power. It required anyone handling drugs to register and pay a tax. No one thought we could ban drugs, but we could regulate and tax them—and a person could only sell or give away heroin or cocaine after filing a form with the IRS. Arguably this law was an abuse of government power, but in those years of reform movements and ill-informed worries about drugs, most didn't mind.

It was also the beginning of an era of progressivism and the Supreme Court was entertaining the idea that the Constitution should be viewed as a "living, breathing" thing that changes as the world turns. Judicial activism for a time became the order of the day as the Court found ways to interpret the Constitution to reach results never imagined by the nation's Founders. The doctrine of "judicial restraint" was adopted. It is a rule imposed by the Court on itself and means the Court defers to Congress so long as the laws it passes are not arbitrary or capricious or contrary to the clear intent of the Constitution. Anyone trying to have a law declared unconstitutional faces the daunting task of persuading the Court that Congress acted with no rational, valid purpose. And so, when Congress and state legislatures adopted anti-drug laws fearing rampant addiction and violent crime it was thought they had a rational purpose in taking away what had earlier been thought a right.

I think the rational basis for today's prohibition of drugs, once strong due to the prevailing ignorance about drugs and addiction, has become weak and is declining to the point that, in time, the Court may be persuaded to call it dead. If Congress won't act to right the wrongs of drug prohibition, maybe down the road the Court will. That would represent a return to Constitutional principle.

The Bill of Rights mandates equal protection of our laws and the non-discriminatory treatment of our people. These concepts are fundamental to our constitutional form of government: our democratic republican form of government. Yet we outlaw recreational drugs, while allowing commercial sales of alcohol, a drug just as addicting as marijuana, heroin or cocaine, and many times more harmful to human health and safety. If an adult wants to use cocaine or heroin instead of the more intoxicating alcohol beverages, what is the reason for the law's discrimination against that preference?

Our law punishes anyone who uses a banned drug, even the addicts whose use, by definition, is out of their control due to changes made in the "wiring" of the brain. Most addicts are people who developed that condition due to a vulnerability they had no way to avoid, plus their use of drugs, at a time before they had the maturity to well evaluate what they were doing. How can it make sense to treat them as criminals? Even though government data show the war on drugs does more harm than good, Congress holds to the belief that it is the only game in town—and so our federal laws against drugs persists. Since we now know it is not the only game in town, a legitimate question is–why?

In the 1925 case of *Linder vs. the United States*, the Supreme Court explained the reach of Congress in the matter of drugs—as it was then understood. The Court pointed out that the Harrison Act's declared object was to collect tax revenue. Congress, they said, cannot pass laws, under the pretext of taxation, for other purposes not entrusted to it by the Constitution. Citing a wealth of prior Court decisions, *Linder* ruled the Act must be construed to avoid doubts of its constitutionality and then said: "Obviously, direct control of medical practice in the states is beyond the power of the federal government." Such control was never delegated to the federal government by the states.

Turning to the Harrison Act, the court noted its prohibition of dispensing opioids or cocaine without a form filed by the receiving person with the Treasury Department–unless given by a doctor for "legitimate medical purposes." Dr. Linder was accused of giving heroin and cocaine pills to an addicted patient facing withdrawal. The patient had not filed the required form. The Court further noted that the Act says nothing about addiction, yet the trial court had found Dr. Linder in criminal violation of the Act because he gave the pills to an addicted person for her comfort. Giving pills to an addict was not thought a legitimate medical purpose, though given to stave off the sickness of withdrawal.

The High Court overturned Dr. Linder's conviction, holding the Act could not be construed constitutionally to prohibit his conduct. The regulation of a medical practice is a state power, not delegated to Congress under the Constitution. Addicts "are diseased and proper subjects for such treatment, and we cannot possibly conclude that a physician acted...for other than medical purposes solely because he has dispensed to one of them...four small tablets of morphine or cocaine for relief of conditions incident to addiction."

So, Dr. Lindner was not guilty, because Congress had no power—and presumably therefore no intention—to regulate his lawful medical practice.

This decision would not occur in today's legal world. Later courts have so broadened Congress's powers that it can regulate about anything it wants. But, this may not be the end of the story. The principle of law relied on by the Court in *Linder* remains firm. A statute must be capable of an interpretation consistent with constitutional guarantees.

Where then, we ask, does the government get the power to outlaw drugs and punish its people who choose in their own pursuit of happiness to use them? It's complicated.

The explanation Congress and the Courts have given up to now is that uncontrolled drug use in society would threaten public health and safety and turn us all into degenerate slovens unable to defend the country or to produce the tax revenues it needs to function. In 1970, when Congress adopted the Controlled Substances Act, we still believed such nonsense. But, not today.

Ignorance and fear of drugs in society have been at the core of our drug policy decisions from the beginning. We know it was wrong to think of drug users as fiends of vampire-like evil. We know that the overwhelming scientific evidence shows drug users are not, in the absence of some underlying mental illness, a delusional and violent bunch. As previously noted, most of those sentenced to prison for various crimes were using drugs at the time of arrest, but there is no empirical evidence for the conclusion that the drugs chemically *caused* their behavior. We know that there is not a general tendency for people to take up drugs. As shown before, regular drug use in the U.S. is practiced by about seven percent of the people and 22 million of the estimated 27 million users just use marijuana. Users of the so-called hard drugs make up less than 2% of us. Most users of all types of drugs, even most addicts, are stable, even productive people. Unlike when our drug laws were enacted, neuroscience today explains brain circuitry and how it changes in addiction, rendering the addicted trapped in a condition from which they will eventually recover, but only with time and challenging effort. Most of us do not believe their behavior should not be judged as if they were ordinary criminals. Today also we have reliable surveys showing that most people shun drugs and of those who use for a time, nearly all quit, even the small minority of users who go on to addiction.

Only a few decades ago, our politicians and many public intellectuals and news media were convinced, however, that prohibiting possession and use of psychoactive drugs for recreational purposes was necessary to protect the nation from crime, violence and the corruption of the people. That, coupled with Supreme Court decisions in the 1930's and 1940's dramatically expanding the reach of the "commerce clause," was enough to justify drug prohibition. The Constitution's commerce clause delegates to Congress the power to regulate commerce between the states. Under a liberal reading of that clause, the Supreme Court gave it wider and wider application to activities we think of as only within a state's borders. Today, nearly any activity you can think of, including buying and selling drugs in the parking lot at Seven-Eleven, has become "interstate commerce." Now all Congress has to do to ban an activity was to find it to be harmful in significant ways.

Over more recent years we have been learning two important realities, already discussed. Drugs are far less dangerous than previously thought, and addiction is mostly the result of adolescent self-medicating to relieve an unhappy life. And it is demonstrably true to say the anti-drug laws have created the black market making drugs available to them. The problems we have with drugs are, in the main, caused–not prevented–by the anti-drug laws—as we showed in Chapter 7.

The feared negatives, which might flow from the toleration of adult drug use, are so outweighed by the harms of our criminal punishment regime it is obvious that we suffer a gross miscarriage of justice of the kind our constitutional traditions have always shunned. This is not to say that some form of regulation is unnecessary or unconstitutional. We should have regulations to avoid leakage of drugs to minors and to promote responsible use and safety. Drug use, other than moderate and responsible use, may interfere with good judgment and endanger others such as when driving skills are compromised. These harmful behaviors can and should be banned. But, the evidence is that none of them has been or can be curtailed by drug prohibition.

On the other hand, a use tolerant system could address all the relevant concerns and provide effective controls. All that stands in the way of that is our federal prohibition. Are we stuck with an old ruling which no longer has a valid, rational purpose, just because the Court is bound to follow precedent? Or might accumulated information provide a basis for the Court to find the old rule no longer justifiable as a legitimate exercise of Congressional power? Let's review what we've got.

After more than a hundred years of prohibition policies and the ills they have brought us, there is no reason to expect business as usual will reverse the failure. The result has been as already discussed, 1) huge burdens on our courts and system of criminal justice, 2) ruination of the careers and lives of tens of thousands of potentially productive people whose offenses were drug related, 3) the inducement to commit property crimes for the money needed to feed the addicts' habits, 4) the fostering of the highly profitable black market and its horrendous violence, 5) the incenting of the business of small time dealers and user/dealers so pervasive and accessible to minors, and 6) the addiction of a couple hundred thousand adolescents each and every year that goes by.

America, indeed the world, recognizes that certain rights are unalienable. Among these are the rights to life, to health, to due process and a fair trial, to be free from torture or cruel, inhuman or degrading treatment, from slavery, and from arbitrary discrimination.

The power of Congress to adopt laws such as those against drug use derives from an interpretation of the "necessary and proper" clause of the Constitution in Article 1, Section 8, clause 18 which reads:

The Congress shall have Power - To make all Laws which shall be necessary and proper for carrying into Execution the foregoing powers and all other Powers vested by this

Constitution in the Government of the United States, or in any Department or Officer thereof.

This "catchall" clause was held by the U.S. Supreme Court in *Gonzales v. Raich,* to be applicable to the commerce clause. In *Raich,* which involved California's medical marijuana law, the Court's majority said:

> Unlike the power to regulate activities that have a substantial effect on interstate commerce, the power to enact laws enabling effective regulation of interstate commerce can only be exercised in conjunction with congressional regulation of an interstate market, and it extends only to those measures necessary to make the interstate regulation effective. … Congress may regulate noneconomic intrastate activities only where the failure to do so "could … undercut" its regulation of interstate commerce. … This is not a power that threatens to obliterate the line between "what is truly national and what is truly local.

Still, the Court found that the growing of marijuana within a state affects the supply and demand balance in the interstate market for the product, and so Congress is in charge. It should be emphasized, however, that the ruling in this case did not address the question of whether there is still a valid, rational purpose in the wielding by Congress of its power. It only addressed whether Congress had such power at the time a law was enacted. A tradition of the Supreme Court is that it defers to Congress on the question of "necessary and proper," but not if it finds an act of Congress to be arbitrary or irrational.

Justice Clarence Thomas, dissented in the *Raich* case and offers a better view, with what to my ear is a finer voice He wrote:

> Respondent's local cultivation and consumption of marijuana is not "Commerce … among the several States." Certainly no evidence from the founding suggests that "commerce" included the mere possession of a good or

some personal activity that did not involve trade or exchange for value. In the early days of the Republic, it would have been unthinkable that Congress could prohibit the local cultivation, possession, and consumption of marijuana....

If the Federal Government can regulate growing a half-dozen cannabis plants for personal consumption (not because it is interstate commerce, but because it is inextricably bound up with interstate commerce), then Congress' Article I powers – as expanded by the Necessary and Proper Clause – have no meaningful limits. Whether Congress aims at the possession of drugs, guns, or any number of other items, it may continue to appropriate state police powers under the guise of regulating commerce....

If the majority is to be taken seriously, the Federal Government may now regulate quilting bees, clothes drives, and potluck suppers throughout the 50 States. This makes a mockery of Madison's assurance to the people of New York that the "powers delegated" to the Federal Government are "few and defined", while those of the States are "numerous and indefinite."

Justice Thomas is here emphasizing the principle of federalism, which promotes experimentation–the very essence of what we need to flourish as a nation. But, *Raich* has upheld the law as a necessary and proper act of Congress under the commerce clause. What can we say to that?

Whether our federal laws against drug use are constitutional today is a potential issue for the court now, because of what we have discovered in recent years. If the court were to take a closer look at the reasons Congress prohibited drugs, and were it to find as a matter of established fact that the Comprehensive Drug Abuse Prevention and Control Act of 1970, which in the beginning passed the test of rational and legitimate purposes, *but no longer does so*, it could find, on that basis, the law is unconstitutional. In other words, if it were found today that the law is no longer suited to its original purpose it could be declared arbitrary or capricious in its effect. Chief Justice Roberts discusses this doctrine in the 2010 case of *Northwest Austin Municipal Utility District Number One vs. Holder,* in which the court held that the doctrine of *stare decisis* (following precedents) does not protect a Congressional statute which is no longer relevant to its supposed purpose.

Let's now turn to another problem with the current law.

Cruel and unusual punishment issues should be considered.

Prohibited punishment is described in the 8th Amendment which states: Excessive bail shall not be required, nor excessive fines imposed, nor cruel and unusual punishments inflicted. In the 1972 case of *Furman vs. Georgia,* the Supreme Court listed four ways a punishment can be considered cruel and unusual:

1. a punishment by its severity is degrading to human dignity especially torture.
2. a severe punishment that is obviously inflicted in wholly arbitrary fashion.
3. a severe punishment that is clearly and totally rejected throughout society.
4. a severe punishment that is patently unnecessary.

As previously discussed, imprisonment is a harsh, degrading, torturous and injurious punishment, though it is not unusual. If it is deserved due to the culpability of the crime, we do not think of it as cruel or unusual within the meaning of the 8th amendment. But whether a punishment is cruel and unusual is often a judgment about whether the punishment fits the crime. Jailing a person for uttering an obscenity would be deemed cruel and unusual even if he uttered it loudly in a public place. We might think differently if he persistently disturbed the peace after warnings and threats of jail time, but a single instance of tasteless speech is no one's idea of a jailable offense. There is what we might call a humanly natural punishment/culpability ratio. We sense a distortion of proportion, whenever the "cruel and unusual" line has been crossed, by comparing the act to the severity of the punishment.

The Supreme Court has also recognized that prison conditions may make a jail sentence cruel and unusual and so unconstitutional. In the 2011 case of *Brown vs. Plata and Coleman* the Court held that prison overcrowding is cruel and unusual punishment in violation of the 8th amendment, even for those sentenced for the worst of crimes. This ruling gives us a sense of what the term means. Cruel and unusual does not refer only to pain or trauma, but includes forms of deprivation beyond acceptable social standards. If overcrowding is an unacceptable deprivation, even for the hardest of criminals, then surely caging a person in the harsh and degrading situation of prison, who has merely used an illegal drug, or possessed one for personal use, is a form of cruel and unusual punishment: one which subjects him or her to the stigma, inhumanity, physical risks and career destroying life interruption. All that for what? Nothing more than enjoying a personal pleasure or relief from anxiety or stress.

Allowing the States to Find the Best Way

As noted above, powers are reserved to the states and to the people unless delegated in the Constitution to the federal government. An advantage of this rule is that each of the fifty states can experiment with untried policies, tweak and perfect them, or abandon them if they fail, and so lead the way for the others. Justice Louis Brandeis long ago put it this way:

> It is one of the happy incidents of the federal system that a single courageous state may, if its citizens choose, serve as a laboratory; and try novel social and economic experiments without risk to the rest of the country.

Given the current U.S. position on drug policy it will likely be necessary for the federal government to enact enabling legislation to pave the way for the System I propose. Let's call it the "Harm Reduction Plan for Scheduled Drug Dispensation Act" or maybe just the "Scheduled Drug Dispensation Act" or "SDDA". This act would alter its prohibitions of the drugs now banned. It would describe the broad outlines of the System and allow state experimentation with programs consistent with it

There will need to be an understanding and cooperation between the states and the federal government with the latter providing policy support while the states and private sector would be providing the operational energy. There would also need to be a continued cooperation between the state law enforcement agencies and the federal officials now common in investigating and interdicting the drug trafficking criminals, gangs and cartels. Competition among the states in formulating and perfecting the System can be expected to enhance that cooperation as more money becomes available from the savings due to reductions in costs of law enforcement, courts and prisons.

The importance of the System's operation by the states and not the federal government cannot be overemphasized. There are differences and variations among the several States and each should retain its sovereign right to administer the program in such way as it deems necessary. Moreover, individual states will be able to make changes to adopt the methods which are seen to work better in other states, or to experiment with new methods of implementation. It is not likely that all states will find the idea agreeable at the start. Not all the original thirteen states signed on to our Constitution initially either. Madison, Hamilton and Jay had to work hard writing the Federalist Papers to persuade New York to sign on and it took North Carolina, Rhode Island and Vermont two more years after that to agree. We should expect dissent and delays and not be discouraged if only some States initially adopt it. But, the logic of the System is compelling and in time reluctant states too will see the benefits of its adoption.

Congress would also need to amend 21 U.S.C. beginning at Section 301 of the US Code, titled the Federal Food, Drug and Cosmetic Act. This law is the statutory scheme under which food, drug, medical devices and other activities relating to human health are regulated. Within this extensive set of rules one finds Section 393, the authorizing statute for the Food and Drug Administration and its purview. The Act is divided into nine subchapters, the ninth being Subchapter IX, Food and Drug Administration. Duties of the FDA are spelled out in subsections (a) through (g), with numerous sub-subsections.

Congress could want to add a subsection (h) which might read as follows:

(h) Oversight and Approval of the Harm Reduction Scheduled Drug Dispensation Plan.

(1) In general

Not later than 1 year after November 21, 2014, the Secretary, after consultation with appropriate scientific and academic experts, health care professionals, representatives of patient and consumer advocacy groups, and the regulated industry, shall develop and publish in the Federal Register a plan under which the Food and Drug Administration will undertake the approval of scheduled drugs for distribution within the meaning of the Federal Harm Reduction Scheduled Drug Dispensation Act, and oversight of and development of appropriate regulations for the implementation of the Plan provided for in said act by and within the several states.

This addition to the Food, Drug and Cosmetics Act would bring under the jurisdiction of the Food and Drug Administration the actual manufacture and approval of the drug products to be dispensed by System operators within the states.

States adopt plan within federal guidelines

Each State would then be able to adopt an experimental or pilot program assuming a cautious first step and would develop needed regulations, and license the appropriate organizations to carry it out. The needs will vary from State to State and within a given state because of wide variations in geographic size, population size and demographics of various locales. It is not practical to try to flesh out the entire program this far in advance of its actual adoption, but, nor should we fear it could be too difficult. We have all the tools we need to pull off the shelf and

Federal registration of operating entities

The companies or special districts who undertake the System operation would also register with the federal government under statutes and regulations already in place. The regulations provide for registration of every person (the word person includes any corporation) who *manufactures, distributes, dispenses, imports, or exports* any controlled substances or who proposes to engage in the manufacture, distribution, dispensing, importation or exportation of a controlled substance. (21 CFR 1300.13) Storage and Security Controls are also detailed and require keeping Schedule I and II drugs such as heroin and cocaine in a separate, approved safe. Specifications for the safe are set forth in the regulations, and the Drug Enforcement Administration Field Office may also be called upon to review proposed security systems. Schedule III-V drugs must also be kept under lock and key, although the choices for what type safe or vault or cage must be used are broader than the rules for Schedule I and II drugs. Recordkeeping is also subject to regulated detail and the records must be kept for two years from the date of the inventory or records. This law can be amended to also regulate the expected large-scale warehousing of drug inventories to be dispensed in the System.

Protection of participant's confidentiality

An important feature of the System is the protection of the participant's confidentiality and privacy. Already in place under Title 42 Public Health (Code of Federal Regulations) which provides detailed restrictions on records of alcohol and drug abuse patient records contains the following:

PART 2—CONFIDENTIALITY OF ALCOHOL AND DRUG ABUSE PATIENT RECORDS

b) *Unconditional compliance required.* The restrictions on disclosure and use in these regulations apply whether the holder of the information believes that the person seeking the information already has it, has other means of obtaining it, is a law enforcement or other official, has obtained a subpoena, or asserts any other justification for a disclosure or use which is not permitted by these regulations.

An amendment would make the necessary adjustment to include the clients of the state chartered operating organizations within the protection of this regulation. Also, as noted earlier, there would need to be provision for a limited disclosure to police officers who make a stop or an arrest on suspicion of illegal drug use in order that the officer could be informed of the status of the arrestee as a client in good standing in the System. Normally the client would carry a card showing his status, but allowance should be made if the card were not in his possession, or its validity questioned, for the officer to confirm through his headquarters that the detainee is a current card holder and authorized to use the particular drug found in his possession.

State Laws and Business Plans

For the System to be given its optimal conditions for success certain principles and requirements will need to be expressed in the enabling legislation. The following are some of these:

1. Control of the scheduled drugs to prevent leakage of them into the hands of minors and other non-participants of the program is of paramount importance.
2. Counselors must be well educated and regularly updated on treatment options available, treatment methods most effective for each drug type and each level of client use, continuously updated on the scientific understandings of drug use risks and how to communicate those facts to the clients, well informed as to protocols to be followed if a client deviates from the rules of the system or becomes a danger to himself or others, and demonstrate knowledge of all facets of the system and its objectives.
3. Counselors must always in their relationships with the clients present themselves as caring, understanding and personable to the maximum extent feasible, treating clients as a medical provider might a patient. Just as doctors do not scold patients who stupidly injure themselves, so the counselor refrains from moral judgment and maintains an ongoing relationship encouraging responsible use. When rules are broken the counselor serves more as a coach who may threaten consequences, but in the way of a caring teacher, not a disciplinarian.
4. The operating entity will employ or contract with licensed medical doctors in sufficient numbers to make a minimum of one physician available to each local office employing ten or more counselors, and one available in each region with counselor staffing of ten so that counselors who discern a need for medical advice for a client will have prompt access to such a physician and will maintain a paid or voluntary medical advisory board to aid the entity in evaluating

operations from a medical viewpoint and advise on best practices to be followed by the counselor staff.

5. Standards of high quality are to be maintained always in respect to employed personnel, facilities, pricing and distribution of drugs and in all aspects of carrying out the purposes of the system.

6. Purchase of drug inventories can be made only from licensed pharmaceutical companies specified by the regulations of its state oversight agency.

7. All forms of drug use promotion would be prohibited.

8. Only those companies will be chartered to operate with a System program that show sufficient capitalization and a viable business plan as shall meet with the approval of the state regulators.

In each state, there will certainly be policy makers, legislative analysts, venture capitalists and business managers who will have additional or better ideas than I have expressed here. The above are spelled out for the purpose of giving the reader an idea of the highly constrained business approach contemplated here.

Chapter 13:

This System Can't Actually Work, Can It?

My pessimism goes to the point of the sincerity of the pessimists.

Edmond Rostand, playwright

Given its coherence and utilization of well- understood processes we should be willing to bet the system will work. There are arguments likely to be raised against it. Let's examine these.

It's unthinkable to allow legitimate pharmaceutical companies to make dangerous drugs

The reaction implied here is normal emotional reaction. It has no factual footing. Setting aside that these drugs are no more "dangerous" than alcohol or any number of other commonly accepted substances, our pharma companies already manufacture opioids and opiates including morphine and heroin, plus amphetamines, cocaine and other mind-altering drugs for use in medical treatment. Morphine is in common use and so are opioid pills that are as potent as heroin. Heroin is used worldwide in the treatment of especially difficult addiction cases. Pain medications, tranquilizers and sleep medications all pose an increased risk of addiction if not carefully used. So, incidentally are sugar are refined wheat flour. Instead of sticking our heads in the sand, we can allow the proposed system to use the resources of drug manufacturers, licensed and regulated by the FDA to make drugs available to adults, who otherwise patronize the illicit trade. The counselors in the system reduce the riskiness of these drugs through monitoring to enforce responsible use. It is beyond question also that the pharmaceutical companies can come up with safer alternatives both in compounds and delivery systems. Under-the-tongue lozenges, for example, could help reduce the riskier snorting and injecting of drugs.

Drug users will not submit to counseling and monitoring.

It is true, of course, that some drug users will recoil at the thought of having to submit to regular and frequent visits and contacts with a professional counselor. To them this may seem too much like being under the scrutiny of probation officers. Inducing users to submit themselves to these controls will likely take time in the case of many, but there are strong incentives for them to join in. Clients of the program will save money, be assured of prompt delivery, know the drugs are as safe as they can be made, and be free of the fear of arrest and incarceration. If a handful of troubled people remain outside the system it will still function as intended to the benefit of the community. The survival of the black market depends on large numbers of customers.

Users will fear the loss of confidentiality

The fear of being outed and socially ostracized will be a major concern to some at the outset. Over time, however, as the benefits become more apparent and our culture begins to view addiction as a treatable medical condition, rather than as criminal conduct, acceptance will increase. Adults who fear for the loss of their jobs or other relationships will likely come to realize that having been offered the choice between acquiring drugs legally and dealing with criminal dealers, the risk of arrest and jail is the less attractive option. It is unlikely society will condone drug use any more than we condone cigarette smoking and so privacy will be important to many clients of the System. The confidentiality provisions will deal with that.

Venture capital will shy from a self-defeating business plan.

If the System is so likely to succeed as I suggest, drug sale revenues to the operating entity should steadily decline as that success materializes. Capital does not seek out businesses that are self-destroying. Financial and business analysts will examine this point closely. If the analysis is that diminishing addiction would eventually end economic viability of operations, then use of the enterprise district type of entity with a tax based revenue stream would likely be the best form of organization. The community it serves will be happy to see it succeed so well it goes out of business. Moreover, there are other revenue producing opportunities for the entity. Some of these were discussed in Chapter 8. It might even morph over time into a community wellness center.

Using in one's home maintains the problem of "cues".

This is certainly a problem for the addicted. However, this problem, notice, is the same as in today's prohibition regime. The System can advise the clients about avoiding cues but it is up to them to organize their lives in the best way they can. However, the dispensary program eliminates the users' need to expose themselves to a whole variety of other cues, especially those associated with all the planning and arranging to get and pay for their drugs. In time, through the coaching they receive, they will develop skills to avoid cues.

Concern for jobs and profits in the treating industry will engender resistance

It is true that as program clients graduate to responsible use, many will move on to quitting without treatment. Moreover, far fewer addictions among adolescents means fewer clients for the addiction treatment industry. Self-interested folks will always oppose measures that might disadvantage them. However, the success of the new System will take time to develop. Treatment providers have little to fear. Moreover, tens of thousands of professional counselors will be needed to staff the various programs within the System. Many in the treating industry are likely to find a welcoming place to employ their skills, though now in coaching responsible use, rather than treating addiction.

Efforts will be made by the cartels and gangs to interfere.

The drug cartels and the gangs that deal drugs are almost certain to try to disrupt operations. This is not a reason to reject the System, but one to hasten its implementation. With each passing year the cartels and gangs grow stronger financially and better able to bribe officials and work at dissuading users from becoming System clients. However, as time passes with the System in place, market forces will weaken them and strengthen us. It's a problem we can deal with.

The absence of criminal sanction means more drug use and social acceptance of it.

As previously discussed, empirical evidence shows this concern is not justified. Moreover, the program operator's role is in part to counsel the clients and includes coaching them to use only moderately and responsibly. The information imparted to them will be far more helpful than what today passes for education and prevention. We can expect with high certainty that drug use will diminish, not increase, as minors are deprived of access to illegal drugs, problematic users stabilize and moderate their use, and the role models and coaching provided by the counselors promote interest in rehab.

Opposition by prison guard unions

Creative destruction is a fact of economic life. As prison populations shrink, because fewer users commit acquisitive crimes to buy drugs, or engage in criminal dealing, some prison guard jobs may disappear. There are other places in our society for trained guards and a new one which will arise in the new System is the need for people to secure the drug inventories. We accept creative destruction of jobs, because no society that resists it can progress economically. The accomplishment of such a great social benefit, as the end of drug prohibition represents, will be politically difficult, but entirely worth the effort.

Children will always be able to get marijuana

Marijuana is grown almost everywhere and can be priced low to keep it affordable as well as available to minors. However, by removing so much of the hard-drug traffic, we allow the police to focus their efforts toward fewer problems. Law enforcement action can be more focused and concentrated on illegal cultivation and sales of marijuana, while working with schools and community officials to better guide the young. There is promise in the System, too, that the counselors in the field will gather and provide information to law enforcement useful to interdiction efforts; not by snitching on clients, but by picking up and passing on information about illegal grow locations and illicit dealer activities. In addition, the program mandates its adult clients avoid leakage of any drug into the hands of children within their sphere of influence. Program controls will predictably improve the situation over what we have now.

Kids will get their drugs from relatives instead of dealers

Teens and sometimes preteens do often get their drugs by pilfering medicine cabinets and the stashes of adults. The control measures of the System aim to curtail this. System clients must commit to handling their drugs responsibly and, in some cases, use the drugs only at locations where children would neither see nor have access to them. Control measures include instructions to the clients on how to secure their drugs, monitoring by the counselor of in-home security measures, and, where deemed necessary, allowing the drug possession only at consumption or injection sites approved by the program. The System time-rations the drugs so that clients who fail to guard their supplies risk running out early: a powerful incentive for addicts to take special care. Clients would be warned that if police or others find their child to have used a drug, their standing in the program will be at risk.

Program operators will try to boost revenues by encouraging drug use.

This concern must and can be dealt with by regulation. It should be remembered, however, that the electric utility companies do not promote unneeded electricity use nor take steps to discourage energy inefficiency; water companies do not advocate wasting water; the dental industry and the medical professions do not encourage unhealthy habits. Regulatory oversight will need to be vigilant, swift and consequential, but there is no reason to fear dominance of perverse incentives in the system.

Chapter 14:

Summation

…policymakers believed that harsh law enforcement action against those involved in drug production, distribution and use would lead to an ever-diminishing market in controlled drugs such as heroin, cocaine and cannabis, and the eventual achievement of a "drug free world." In practice, the global scale of illegal drug markets—largely controlled by organized crime—has grown dramatically over this period.

Global Commission on Drug Policy

More than a hundred years after we first started trying to curb drugs by outlawing them, we suffer with all the same problems, but with their persistent growth in magnitude each year. Law enforcement is not equipped with the magic formula they would need to succeed. It is time we understand the issues and conform public policy to reality.

While most users of drugs, including addicts, got their start as adolescents, a super-majority of users are adults in their 20s and 30s—more than twenty million of them. Some drug addiction forms among older adults—often pain patients who were prescribed opioid pills, then later turned to cheaper and easier-to-get heroin. That huge adult drug use market is where the traffickers and dealers maker their money. And those are the crooks who make drugs also available to minors. We cannot end the persistent propagation of new drug users and addicts, until we end the adult market opportunities for the traffickers. Do that and you kill the drug trade. Killing the illegal drug trade would accomplish an impressive list of beneficial changes in our world. That will only happen when new laws tolerate the regulated adult use of legal drugs.

The laws against drugs are impotent against drug dealing and use.

Law enforcement resources are not sufficient to discover and apprehend all the money-motivated farmers, producers, large traffickers, dealers and user/dealers of illegal drugs. The drug king- pins, their lieutenants and distributors are so well funded, armed and sophisticated that border patrols and ordinary police work has been unable to stop them. And, the small-scale dealers are so numerous and pervasive the police have never found a way to cage enough of them to make a significant difference. With trucks, planes, boats and human "mules" at their disposal, the traffickers boast they can move drug products across our borders at will.

The skills and professionalism of our various federal, state and local agencies are not here questioned. The commonplace instances of corrupt officials and cops should not taint the majority of enforcement personnel. And it is sad to think that our laws against drugs are providing the inducements for the corruptible few who sully the honor of the many. But, bribes and intimidation of the few are just a cost of doing business for the smugglers. The notion that all we need to do is put our best minds to work on figuring out how to catch, to interdict, to jail the dealers, and rehabilitate the drug users is nothing more than a fading, unrealistic hope. There is so much money to be made, the market rules.

We are waging an inhumane war against ourselves.

The movie Traffic, tells a story based in part on actual events occurring about 1997, involving DEA agents and Mexican police and officials pitted against the overwhelmingly powerful drug cartels. It portrays the corruption, murdering and torturing that go on in the drug trade and the easy access of our young to judgment impairing drugs, for which the ultimate blame must come back to our ill-conceived war on drugs. Though the film is a dramatization with a viewpoint, it does not, overstate those horrors. Near its end the newly appointed national "Drug Czar" (played by Michael Douglas) begins to read an opening statement at his first press conference. His intention is to present a strongly worded statement describing his commitment to an aggressive effort to win the war on drugs. Unfortunately, he has recently discovered his own sixteen-year-old daughter is allowing herself to be sexually exploited in exchange for drugs. He starts his statement, but then faltering his reading slows and conviction in what he is saying disappears. Only a few sentences into his speech, he stops, looks at the audience of reporters and asks: "How can we make war against our own families?" Then with head lowered he murmurs "I can't do this" and walks out of the building with a new purpose: to find his child and save her life.

Based upon all that we have discussed in the chapters of this book, how can we as adults and parents not come to the same conclusion? Our "war" only attacks our people. It does not destroy either the seeming need of some of us to use drugs, or the ability of the underworld to supply them.

Realistic expectations for the System

Let us also acknowledge that there are predictable challenges. Some clients of the System will not be suitably cooperative people. Some will be difficult to work with. And there will be those who try to game the System, who cheat and violate the rules and those who go right on committing crime the way they did before. Still, the huge majority of drug users and addicts are decent citizens who are likely to follow the rules of the System. And we can learn to cope with the problems posed by those who deviate. Meanwhile, by killing the illegal trade and depriving children of their current easy access to drugs we will gradually reduce the problem of the rule breakers to the barest minimum. Trial and experimentation and the flexible responses to the discovery of overlooked possibilities and surprise developments will shape the concept to its optimum form. We can predict the tangible benefits to be realized.   Let's review them.

1. Dry up the black market so accessible to the young—a market that brings crime and violence to nearly every community.
2. Control leakage of drugs into the hands of children, and both teach and insist upon responsible use by adults entrusted with their care and upbringing.
3. End the many harms of incarcerating drug users, which include depriving children of their incarcerated parents, interrupting the career development of young adults, dehumanizing and stigmatizing men and women with productive potential and ruining their employment prospects, subjecting these people to the risks of prison violence and overcrowding, wasting human capital and serving as a crime school for young adults.
4. Provide the alternative use to adults of legally manufactured drugs which are certified as to chemical purity and potency.
5. Identify and maintain contact with most if not all drug users and addicts through trained counselors who work with them to teach and insist upon responsible use, provide them the information they need, and encourage them to create for themselves the conditions that aid the process of addiction recovery.
6. Reduce each State's law enforcement, incarceration and probation costs by many billions of dollars annually;

7. Because of #6, free up funds to finance increased education of both adults and youths about drugs, and help identify and work with at-risk youths.
8. Produce increased funding for treatment programs, research and development of medical solutions in aid of addiction recovery and for media campaigns to educate the public about risks of drug use;
9. End the inducement of addicted users to commit crimes to pay for their drugs, and so further increase community safety and reducing crime related costs.
10. Reduce and eventually end the corruption of officials and police officers engaged in drug law enforcement;

A system which promotes each and all the above is one that deserves the enthusiastic support of the entire nation. The System described here aligns public drug policy with human nature and the power of the marketplace. For these reasons, its success is highly likely wherever and on whatever territorial scale it is installed.

System as pragmatic and principled

We as a nation, and a people, who lead the world in its progression toward greater humanity, scientific and social knowledge, along with the means to produce the wealth and the freedom to deploy it, will continue in our progress and leadership if we keep our focus on our true interests. Those interests lie in the health and productivity of our people. The System is a pragmatic, but also a principled approach. Its underlying principle is that people troubled with mental disorders, which drug addiction certainly is, are to be helped, not punished. It is a call to abandon a decades-old, tried, failed and often inhumane methodology. It aims to rid our country and the world of irresponsible abuse of drugs, along with the cartels and street gangs and their associated crime and violence.

To understand the System in all its detail is to see it as a concrete, coherent, and practical approach to changing the framework of the underworld business model, which profits from adults and supplies drugs to the young so vulnerable to addiction.

I hope dear reader that you will help me to promote and win acceptance for this System, for that will facilitate progress toward a drug responsible America, a model for humanity.

Suggested Reading

Balko, R., (2013) *Rise of the Warrior Cop: The Militarization of America's Police Forces*, Public Affairs, New York,

Gray, M., (2000) *Drug Crazy: How We Got into This Mess and How We Can Get Out of It* Routledge, New York, NY

Hari, J. (2015) *Chasing the Scream,* N.Y., New York, Bloomsbury

Hart, C., (2013) *High Price, A Neuroscientist's Journey of Self Discovery That Challenges Everything You Know about Drugs and Society*

Heyman, G. *Addiction: A Disorder of Choice,* (2009) Harvard University Press, Cambridge, MA

Husak, D. (1992) *Drugs and Rights,* New York, N.Y. Cambridge Univ. Press

Husak, D., & Marneffe, P., (2005) *Legalizing Drugs* New York, NY Cambridge Univ. Press

Kleiman, M. A. R., Caulkins, J.P. &Hawken, A., (2011) *Drugs and Drug Policy,* New York, NY, Oxford Univ. Press

Lewis, M., (2015) *The Biology of Desire,* Phil. PA, Public Affairs (Perseus)

Maté, G. (2010) *In the Realm of the Hungry Ghosts,* Berkeley, CA North Atlantic Books

Satel, S., & Lilienfeld, S.O., (2013) *Brainwashed. The Seductive Appeal of Mindless Neuroscience,* New York NY, Basic Books

Slater, Dan, (2016) *Wolf Boys* New York, NY, Simon & Shuster

Szalavitz, M., (2016) *Unbroken Brain,* N.Y. New York, St. Martins Press

References

[1] Global Commission on Drug Use, (2011) Executive Summary http://www.globalcommissionondrugs.org/wp-content/themes/gcdp_v1/pdf/Global_Commission_Report_English.pdf

[2] Lancet Commissions, (2016) Public health and international drug policy Retrieved from: http://www.thelancet.com/pdfs/journals/lancet/PIIS0140-6736(16)00619-X.pdf

[3] Becker, G., (2005) The Failure of the War on Drugs, Retrieved from: http://www.becker-posner-blog.com/2005/03/the-failure-of-the-war-on-drugs-becker.html

[4] According the National Center for Addiction and Substance Abuse (CASA) 90% of all addictions stem from initiation of use between the ages of 12 and 17. Dr. Carl Hart states that between 10% and 20% of those who initiate drug use become addicted. Dr. Nora Volkow, et. al. of NIDA state that vulnerability to addiction is greatest during the adolescent years.

[5] CASA (2012) Retrieved from https://www.centeronaddiction.org/newsroom/press-releases/national-study-reveals-teen-substance-use-america%E2%80%99s-1-public-health-problem

[6] Ibid.

[7] Maté, G. (2010) *In the Realm of the Hungry Ghosts*, Berkeley, CA North Atlantic Books

8 Volkow, N., Koob, G.F., McLellan, A.N., (2016)) Neurobiologic Advances from the Brain Disease Model of Addiction., NEJM, accessed 11/8/2016 at http://www.nejm.org/doi/full/10.1056/NEJMra1511480#t=article

9 Volkow, et. al. Ibid.

10 Volkow, et. al. Ibid.

11 Hart, C.L., and Ksir, C., (2015) *Drugs, Society & Human Behavior* (16th ed.) New York, N.Y. McGraw Hill pp 34-40.

12 Hart and Ksir, Ibid.

13 American Psychiatric Association, (2013) Diagnostic and Statistical Manual of Mental Disorders, 5th Edition: DSM-5: Substance Use Disorder

14 For an instructive treatment of this phenomenon see Korb, A., (2015) *The Upward Spiral* Oakland, CA New Harbinger Publications, p 70 et. seq.

15 Satel, S., & Lilienfeld, S.O., (2013) *Brainwashed. The Seductive Appeal of Mindless Neuroscience*, New York NY, Basic Books, Chapter 3.

16 Hart and Ksir, Ibid. p 42.

17 Amsterdam Info., Amsterdam Drugs Policy. Information accessed 7/10/2017 at https://www.amsterdam.info/drugs/

18 Satel & Lilienfeld, Ibid. See also Kleiman, M. A. R., Caulkins, J.P. &Hawken, A., (2011) *Drugs and Drug Policy,* New York, NY, Oxford Univ. Press, p 95.

19 Gray, Mike. (2000) *Drug Crazy: How We Got into This Mess and How We Can Get Out of It.* Routledge, NY, pp 54,55. Gray is an acclaimed film writer. I rely here on this well sourced history of the drug war. He is not to be confused with Judge James Gray whose book is later cited herein.

20 Satel & Lilienfeld, Ibid

[21] Husak, D. (1992) *Drugs and Rights,* New York, N.Y. Cambridge Univ. Press, pp 27-37

[22] Manski, F., Pepper, J.V., (2001*) Informing America's Policy on Illegal Drugs: What We Don't Know Keeps Hurting Us,* Commission on Behavioral and Social Sciences and Education (CBASSE) p.17

[23] Gray, M. Ibid.

[24] Gray, M. Ibid.

[25] Miron, J.A. (2004) *Drug War Crimes,* Oakland, CA, The Independent Institute, p 38

[26] Gray, M. Ibid.

[27] Gray, M. Ibid.

[28] As quoted by McNamara, J. Evaluating the National Strategies of Drug Control, (2011) LEAP Publications, Retrieved from: http://www.leap.cc/evaluating-the-national-strategies-of-drug-control/

[29] Gray, M. Ibid.

[30] Gray, M. Ibid.

[31] O'Grady, M.A. (2013) Bolivia's Descent into Rogue State Status, Wall Street Journal, 10/28/2013, Retrieved from http://online.wsj.com/news/articles/SB10001424052702304069604579158293350301588?mod=ITP_opinion_0

[32] The 2017 report of the United Nations Office on Drugs and Crime shows a 25% increase in coca production in the years 2013-15. GLOBAL OVERVIEW OF DRUG DEMAND AND SUPPLY, Booklet 2. Retrieved from: file:///C:/Users/drfin/AppData/Roaming/Zotero/Zotero/Profiles/o0yx3344.default/zotero/storage/XKW6N3M8/Booklet_2_HEALTH.pdf

[33] For a graphic portrayal of how ambitious drug entrepreneurs out-smart law enforcement on both sides of our southern border see *Wolf Boys,* by Dan Slater (2016) New York, N.Y., Simon & Schuster

[34] Transform, (2017) UK Government Official Evaluation: Our Drug Strategy is a failure (but Home Office carry on anyway) Retrieved from http://www.tdpf.org.uk/blog/uk-government-official-evaluation-our-drug-strategy-failure-home-office-carry-anyway

[35] Wall Street Journal, August 12, 2013: "Obama Administration Plans Overhaul to Cut Prison Population"

[36] Miron, J.A., Ibid

[37] Jacobs, A., (2010) China Turns Drug Rehab into a Punishing Ordeal, NYT, January 7, 2010

[38] Transform (2017) Ibid.

[39] SAMHSA, (2016) Behavioral Health Trends in the United States: Results from the 2014 National Survey on Drug Use and Health, Retrieved from https://www.samhsa.gov/data/sites/default/files/NSDUH-FRR1-2014/NSDUH-FRR1-2014.pdf

[40] Satel, S. (2016) Shortcuts to Addiction WSJ Accessed 3/3/2017 at: https://www.wsj.com/articles/shortcuts-to-addiction-1481153114

[41] Report of Global Commission on Drug Use. June 2011, http://www.globalcommissionondrugs.org/reports.

[42] Luhnow, D., (2012) Mexico Drug Violence Shows Decline., Wall Street Journal dtd. 6/14/2012

[43] Kleiman, Caulkins, Hawken, (2011) Drugs and Drug Policy: What Everyone Needs to Know, New York, N.Y., Oxford University Press,

References

[44] Husak, D., & Marneffe, P., (2005) *Legalizing Drugs* New York, NY Cambridge Univ. Press

[45] Gray, J. (2001) Why Our Drug Laws Have Failed and What We Can Do About It, Philadelphia, PA, Temple University Press pp. 43-4

[46] Gray, J. Ibid pp. 134-5

[47] ONDCP blog post by Kerlikowske and Jealous, Toward a Smarter Drug Policy, February 14, 2013, http://www.whitehouse.gov/blog/2013/02/14/toward-smarter-drug-policy

[48] Kleiman, M., *Where Brute Force Fails*, Princeton, Univ. Press, N.J. 2009, p. 111.

[49] Balko, R., (2013) Rise of the Warrior Cop: The Militarization of America's Police Forces, Public Affairs, New York, Kindle ed. Location 4340-47 to 5585-98 In his chapter titled "2000s –Whole New War" Balko cites numerous examples of the nightmare experience of innocent victims of overly aggressive police action.

[50] JAMA, March 10, 2004—Vol 291, No. 10 Data are from McGinnis and Foege.

[51] Centers for Disease Control, (2017) Opioid Overdose, Retrieved from: https://www.cdc.gov/drugoverdose/index.html

[52] Gray, James P. *Why Our Drug Laws Have Failed.* Ibid.

[53] Wall Street Journal "Chicago Hunts for Answers to Gang Killings" July 13, 2012

[54] Williamson, Kevin, "Gangsterville", National Review, Feb. 25, 2013

[55] Balko, Ibid. Kindle ed. Location 4340-47

56 Balko, Ibid. Kindle ed. Locations 4339-46 and 4491-98

57 Miron, J.A. Ibid. pp 36,7

58 UNODC (2011) Report, Executive Summary, Retrieved from http://
www.unodc.org/documents/data-and-analysis/WDR2011/World_
Drug_Report_2011_ebook.pdf

59 See World Drug Report, 2012 Executive Summary, http://www.unodc.
org.

60 SAMHSA, (2016) Ibid.

61 "'Bath Salts' Pose a Hurdle for Prosecutors", Wall Street Journal,
August 15, 2013

62 For a detailed description of the black tar market see Quinone, S.,
Dreamland New York, NY, Bloomsbury Press

63 International Harm Reduction Association (2010)   What Is Harm
Reduction, English.pdf. Retrieved from http://www.ihra.net/
files/2010/08/10/Briefing_What_is_HR_English.pdf

64 An explanatory video on YouTube shows this operation and explains the
importance of bringing severely addicted people into the fold of caring
helpful health workers. (2016) "Vancouver's First Supervised Injection Site"
Accessed 6/5/2017 at https://www.youtube.com/watch?v=Yw1BIJqUz4s

65 See the information rich article on Wikipedia, Insite, accessed
6/3/2017 at: https://en.wikipedia.org/wiki/Insite

66 Dr. Brandon Marshall, (2016) 3 million drug injections and zero
deaths? How is that possible? You Tube video accessed 6/5/2017 at
https://www.youtube.com/watch?v=ufzaTQiNBr4&t=8s

67 The Seattle Times, (2017) As Seattle eyes supervised drug-injection
sites, is Vancouver a good model? Accessed 6/8/2017 at: http://

www.seattletimes.com/seattle-news/health/is-vancouvers-safe-drug-use-site-a-good-model-for-seattle/

[68] Wright, N., Tomkins, N., (2004) Supervised Injection Centers BMJ. 2004 Jan 10; 328(7431): 100–102.
doi: 10.1136/bmj.328.7431.100 Retrieved from: https://www.ncbi.nlm.nih.gov/pmc/articles/PMC314055/

[69] Diep, F. (2016) Inside North America's Only Legal Safe Injection Facility, Pacific Standard, Accessed 6/7/2017 at https://psmag.com/news/inside-north-americas-only-legal-safe-injection-facility

[70] NCBI (2010) Vancouver's supervised injection facility challenges Canada's drug laws, Accessed 6/8/2017 at: https://www.ncbi.nlm.nih.gov/pmc/articles/PMC2942917/

[71] Satel, S., (2017) Saving Lives Is the First Imperative in the Opioid Epidemic WSJ, Retrieved from https://www.wsj.com/articles/saving-lives-is-the-first-imperative-in-the-opioid-epidemic-1491768767

[72] Greenwald, G., (2009) Drug Decriminalization in Portugal, CATO Institute. Retrieved from http://www.cato.org/publications/white-paper/drug-decriminali…l-drug-policies

[73] See excellent and detailed discussion in Hari, Johann, (2015) *Chasing the Scream*, N.Y., New York, Bloomsbury

[74] National Association of Drug Court Professionals (2013) What are Drug Courts? Retrieved from http://www.nadcp.org/learn/what-are-drug-courts

[75] This is the experience of a100 Texas state drug courts according to Right on Crime, "Substance Abuse" retrieved from http://rightoncrime.com/category/priority-issues/substance-abuse/

[76] Peele, S., Bufe, C., and Brodsky, A., (2000) Resisting 12-Step Coercion, Tucson, AR, Sharp Press

[77] Fletcher, A., (2013) Inside Rehab: The Surprising Truth About Addiction Treatment – and How to Get Help that Works, New York, NY, Viking Penguin, Kindle ed. Location 3450 et seq.

[78] Szalavitz, M., (2016) Unbroken Brain, N.Y. New York, St. Martins Press

[79] Fletcher, A., (2013) Ibid. Kindle ed. Location 3469 et seq.

[80] Satel and Lilienfeld, (2013) Ibid.

[81] Satel and Lilienfeld, (2013) Ibid.

[82] Gelb, A., (2009) Washington Post, July 13, 2009

[83] Gelb, A., Ibid.

[84] McNamara, J.P. (2012) Interview with Dean Becker, 2012, http://www.drugtruth.net/cms/node/3931

[85] Hollersen, W., (2013) This Is Working': Portugal, 12 Years after Decriminalizing Drugs, translation from German by Ornstein, E., Spiegel Online International, retrieved at http://www.spiegel.de/international/europe/evaluating-drug-decriminalization-in-portugal-12-years-later-a-891060.html
http://www.spiegel.de/international/europe/evaluating-drug-decriminalization-in-portugal-12-years-later-a-891060.html

[86] Hollersen, W. Ibid.

[87] Hollersen, W. Ibid.

[88] Cussen, M., & Block, W., (2000) Legalize Drugs Now. The American Journal of Economics and Sociology, Vol 59, No. 3

[89] Duke, S.B. (1993) How Drug Legalization Would Cut Crime, LA Times

[90] The Week Online, (1995) "Police Chiefs Question Merits of Drug War Policies" Retrieved from http://www.drcnet.org/cops/question.html

[91] Police Foundation, A National Survey Among Chiefs of Police, research by Peter D. Hart Res. Assoc. December 2004

[92] The citation for these quotes in the 1st edition of this book was in error, and I have not been able to recover the correct cite. However, an internet search turns up any number of statements by Stamper consistent with this.

[93] Volkow, et. al. Ibid.

[94] Maté, G. Ibid.

[95] Husak, D., & de Marneffe, P., (2005) *The Legalization of Drugs (For and Against)*, Cambridge, NY, Cambridge Univ. Press,

[96] Gray, J., (2011) *Why Our Drug Laws Have Failed, and What We Can Do About It.*, Phil. PA, Temple Univ. Press

[97] Report of Global Commission on Drug Policy, (2011) Executive Summary, Retrieved from http://www.globalcommissionondrugs.org/wp-ontent/themes/gcdp_vl/pdf/Global_Commission_Report_English.pdf

[98] Report of Global Commission on Drug Policy, Ibid

[99] Bobo, L.D. & Thompson, V., (2006) Unfair by Design: The War on Drugs, Race, and the Legitimacy of the Criminal Justice System, Social Research: Vol 73: No 2

[100] Thernstrom, S., & Thernstrom, A. (2013) The Status of the Dream, National Review Vol. LXV, No. 17, p.28

[101] Tuttle, I. (2013) "Justice for the System" National Review Vol. LXV, No. 15 p. 32. Accessed 6/28/2017 at: http://www.nationalreview.com/article/393741/justice-system-ian-tuttle

[102] Tuttle, Ibid.

[103] Tuttle, Ibid.

104 Husak, D., & de Marneffe, P., Ibid.

105 Kennedy, P.J., (2013) Project SAM (Smart Approaches to Marijuana) joined by American Academy of Pediatrics, Colorado chapter, National Association of Drug Court Professionals, Community, Anti-Drug Coalitions of America, National Narcotics Officers Associations Coalition, Smart Colorado. The letter can be viewed at www. http://learnaboutsam.com/wp-content/uploads/2013/02/FEB-KENNEDY-LETTER-DOJ.pdf

106 DuPont, L.D., Bensinger, P. & Blue, L., (Letter to the Editor, January 15, 2013) Wall Street Journal

107 Kleiman, M. A.R., Caulkins, J.P., Hawken, A., (2011) *Drugs and Drug Policy*, New York, NY, Oxford Univ. Press, pp. 198-200

108 1 Kerlikowske, R., G. & Jealous, T., (February 14, 2013) Toward a Smarter Drug Policy, Retrieved from http://www.whitehouse.gov/blog/2013/02/14/toward-smarter-drug-policy

109 Bennett, Dilulio, Walters, *Body Count, New* York, Simon & Schuster, 1995 pp. 140-41.

110 Gray, J.P., (2001) Ibid. p 222

111 Woodruff, B., (2013) Rocky Mountain High, National Review, Vol. LXV, No.17, p. 25

112 Kevin Sabet debates former NM Governor Gary Johnson at Yale in a YouTube video. Accessed 6/10/2017 at: https://www.youtube.com/watch?v=VABQ-XovTU0

113 Morin, J. (2004) *Drug War Crimes*, Oakland, CA, The Independent Institute, p 72

114 Hart, C. (2013), *High Price, A Neuroscientist's Journey of Self Discovery That Challenges Everything You Know About Drugs and Society*, New York, NY, Harper Collins, Kindle ed. Location 248-54

[115] Volkow, et. al. Ibid.

[116] SAMHSA Ibid.

[117] Miron, J., ibid. p.62

[118] Becker, G., (2005) The Failure of the War on Drugs-BECKER, retrieved from: http://www.becker-posner-blog.com/2005/03/the-failure-of-the-war-on-drugs-becker.html

[119] United States Government Accountability Office, (2012) U.S. Agencies Have Allotted Billions in Andean Countries, but DOD Should Improve Its Reporting of Results, GAO-12-824

[120] Belenko, S., & Peugh, J., (Fall,1998) Fighting Crime by Treating Substance Abuse, Issues in Science and Technology Online, Retrieved from http://www.issues.org/15.1/belenk.htm

[121] Masters, J. (2012) Why the Fiscal Health of States and Cities Matters, Council on Foreign Relations, Retrieved from http://www.cfr.org/economics/why-fiscal-health-states-cities-matters/p291-98

[122] Masters, J. Ibid.

[123] Prescott, E., (2004) Why Do Americans Work So Much More Than Europeans? FEDERAL RESERVE BANK OF MINNEAPOLIS Quarterly Review vol. 28, No 1, Retrieved from: https://www.minneapolisfed.org/research/qr/qr2811.pdf

[124] Hart, C. (2012) *High Price, New York, NY,* Harper-Collins, Kindle ed. Locations 240-46, 246-51.
SAMSHA, NSDUH (2012) Results from the 2011 National Survey on Drug Use and Health:
Summary of National Findings Series H-44, Publication no. 12-4713.

[125] Volkow, et. al. Ibid.

[126] Satel/Lilienfeld, Ibid.

[127] Randazzo, S. (2017) Law Firms Finally Say It's OK to See a Therapist, WSJ, Retrieved from: https://www.wsj.com/articles/law-firms-finally-say-its-ok-to-see-a-therapist-1495381847

[128] NCADD, (2015) Alcohol, Drugs and Crime, Retrieved from: https://www.ncadd.org/about-addiction/alcohol-drugs-and-crime. And see J.A. Miron, J.A. (2004) *Drug War Crimes*, Oakland, CA, Independent Inst. p 15, and sources there cited.

[129] Kahneman, D. (2011) *Thinking, Fast and Slow*, Farrar, New York, NY, Strauss, and Giroux, N.Y. pp. 137-45

[130] Kahneman, D. (2011) Ibid.

[131] Krause, K., (2013) The Progressive War on Science, eSkeptic, http://www.skeptic.com/eskeptic/13-03-13

[132] Husak, D., (1992)   *Drugs and Rights*, New York, NY, Cambridge Univ. Press, p 63

[133] Pew Research Center (2013) Majority Now Supports Legalizing Marijuana, Pew Research Center, http://www.people-press.org/2013/04/04/majority-now-supports-legalizing-marijuana/

[134] Volkow, et. al. Ibid.

[135] Phillips, E.E. & Kesling, B., (2013) Some Church Folk Ask: 'What Would Jesus Brew?' Wall Street Journal, WSJ, 3/9/2013

[136] Gray, M., (2000), *Drug Crazy, New* York, N.Y. Routledge, p.52

[137] Satel, S., & Lilienfeld, S.O., (2013) Ibid.

[138] Centers for Disease Control and Prevention (2010) Attention-deficit/Hyperactivity Disorder, Retrieved from http://www.cdc.gov/ncbddd/adhd/data.html

[139] Lewis, M., (2015) *The Biology of Desire*, Phil. PA, Public Affairs (Perseus) Kindle ed., loc. 61

[140] As quoted by Steve Rolles, (2007) *After the War on Drugs; Tools for the Debate*, Transform Drug Policy Foundation, http: www.tdpf.org.uk.

[141] Phelps, E.S. (2007) Economic Dynamism and the "Social Market Economy:" Are they Reconcilable? Ludwig-Erhard-Lecture, http://www.columbia.edu/~esp2/ErhardLectureBerlin2007Oct12FriLast.pdf

[142] McAfee, A., Brynjolfsson, E., *Machine, Platform, Crowd*, New York, NY, W.W. Norton

[143] Kleiman, M., (Winter,1998) "Middle Ground" UCLA Magazine

[144] CASA: https://www.centeronaddiction.org/newsroom/press-releases/national-study-reveals-teen-substance-use-america%E2%80%99s-1-public-health-problem

[145] CASA (2012) Retrieved from https://www.centeronaddiction.org/addiction-research/reports/national-survey-american-attitudes-substance-abuse-teens-2012

[146] Blakemore, S., (2012) The mysterious workings of the adolescent brain TED, Accessed 1/13/2017 at: https://www.ted.com/talks/sarah_jayne_blakemore_the_mysterious_workings_of_the_adolescent_brain/transcript?language=en

[147] Venturelli, P., (January 2000) Drugs in Schools: Myths and Realities, Annals of American Academy of Political and Social Science, Vol.567. No.72, pp. 72-87

[148] Venturelli, Ibid.

[149] Volkow, N. et. al. Ibid.

150 Venturelli, Ibid pp.72-87

151 Volkow, N., et. al. Ibid.

152 Satel, S., Lilienfeld, S. (2013) Ibid.

153 Satel. S., Lilienfeld, S. (2013) Ibid.

154 Heyman, G., (2009) *Addiction: A Disorder of Choice*, Cambridge, MA, Harvard U. Press p114

155 Lewis, M. (2015) *The Biology of Desire: Why Addiction is Not a Disease.* United States, Public Affairs-Perseus Kindle ed. Loc. 69.

156 Satel, S., Lilienfeld, S. (2013) Ibid.

157 Korb, A., (2015) *Upward Spiral,* Oakland, CA, New Harbinger, p 68

158 Lewis, M. (2015) Ibid.

159 Szalavitz, M., (2016) *Unbroken Brain*, N.Y. New York, St. Martins Press

160 Maté, G. (2010) *In the Realm of Hungry Ghosts*, Berkeley, CA, North Atlantic Books

161 Satel, S. & Lilienfeld, S. (2013) Ibid.

162 Hart, C. (2013) Ibid.

163 Satel &Lilienfeld, (2013) Ibid.

164 Satel & Lilienfeld, Ibid. See also Lewis, M., (2015) Ibid.

165 Fletcher, A. Ibid.

166 Szalavitz, M. Ibid. p 193

167 Lewis, M., (2015) Ibid.

References

[168] Laudet, A.B. (2003) Attitudes and Beliefs About 12-Step Groups Among Addiction Treatment Clients and Clinicians: Toward Identifying Obstacles to Participation, NIH Public Access, retrieved from http://www.ncbi.nlm.nih.gov/pubmed/14677780 The authors acknowledge that convenience of access to the group and scheduling times of the meetings also bear upon an individual's participation rate and likely success in recovery.

[169] Peele, S., Bufe, C., and Brodsky, A., (2000) Resisting 12-Step Coercion, Tucson, AR, Sharp Press Kindle ed. Location 490 et. seq. The authors consider the 12-Step treatment of alcohol and scheduled drug addictions as essentially similar and show that 12-Step efficacy is no better than and may be inferior to a variety of other recovery approaches including spontaneous recovery. See also Fletcher, A. Ibid. Location 1421 et. seq.

[170] This interview was conducted by the author in May 2013, in Nevada City, CA. As noted elsewhere, completion of drug court programs does not necessarily prove addiction recovery. Some of the completers, maybe a large percentage of them, will relapse yet manage to avoid return to court.

[171] Kleiman, M.A.R. (2012) Dopey, Boozy, Smoky –And Stupid, The American Interest Magazine, Retrieved from http://www.the-american-interest.com/article.cfm?piece=224 p 7

[172] Kleiman, Ibid p 4

[173] Bakalar, Nicholas, Review Sees No Advantage in 12-Step Programs, NY Times, July 25, 2006

[174] Bakalar, et al., Ibid

[175] Bakalar, et al., Ibid

[176] Bakalar, et al., Ibid

[177] Fletcher, A. Ibid Location 5647-545651-46

[178] Fletcher, A. Ibid Location 3021-26

[179] Fletcher, A., Ibid Location 2978 et seq.

[180] Fletcher, A., Ibid. Location 3073-83

[181] Wessel, D. "Gaming the System to Beat Rush Hour Traffic, Wall Street Journal, 8/1/2013

[182] Wessel, D. Ibid.

[183] Volkow, et. al., (2017) Ibid.

[184] Transform, (2017) Heroin-assisted treatment in Switzerland: successfully regulating the supply and use of a high-risk injectable drug, Retrieved from: http://www.tdpf.org.uk/blog/heroin-assisted-treatment-switzerland-successfully-regulating-supply-and-use-high-risk-0

[185] Anderson, D., NIDA NOTES, Retrieved from: https://www.drugabuse.gov/news-events/nida-notes/2016/04/narrative-discovery-in-search-medication-to-treat-methamphetamine-addiction-part-2

[186] MedlinePlus, (2013) Diet and Substance Abuse Recovery, Retrieved from http://www.nlm.nih.gov/medlineplus/ency/article/002149.htm

[187] Satel and Lilienfeld, (2013) Ibid

[188] Volkow, et. al. Ibid.

[189] Kleiman, M.A.R., Ibid; Fletcher, A.M. Ibid. Fletcher is the New York Times health and medical writer. In this book, she writes: "It seems to be a well-kept secret, however, that most people overcome alcohol and drug problems without ever setting foot in an addiction treatment program."

[190] Moore, M.H., & Kleiman, M. A.R., (1989) The Police and Drugs, National Institute of Justice, U.S. Department of Justice, and the Program in Criminal Justice Policy and Management, John F. Kennedy

School of Government, Harvard University. No.11 https://www.ncjrs.gov/pdffiles1/nij/117447.pdf

[191] American Council for Drug Education, Basic Facts About Drugs: Ecstasy http://westmoreland.pa.networkofcare.org/mh/library/article.aspx?id=922

[192] National Institute on Drug Abuse, Infofax on Heroin No. 13548 as recited by Get the Facts, War on Drugs.Org http://www.drugwarfacts.org/cms/node/58.

[193] CDC Drug Overdose Death Data Retrieved from https://www.cdc.gov/drugoverdose/data/statedeaths.html

[194] Frontline. Retrieved from http://www.pbs.org/wgbh/pages/frontline/meth/faqs/

[195] Center for Disease Control and Prevention: Accessed 5/16/2017 at https://www.cdc.gov/hiv/risk/idu.html.

[196] Vimont, C., (2013) Using Bath Salts: Playing Russian Roulette with Your Brain, Expert Says" http://www.drugfree.org/join-together

[197] Dalton, M., (2013) EU Seeks Action on 'Legal Highs', Wall Street Journal, U.S. Edition 9/17/2013 p A12

[198] Woodruff, B., (2013) Rocky Mountain High, National Woodruff Review, Vol. LXV, No.17, p. 25,26

[199] Levitt, S. (2007) The Freakonomics of McDonalds You Tube Video, accessed 6/5/17 at https://www.youtube.com/watch?v=5UGC2nLnaes

[200] Moore & Kleiman, Ibid.

[201] Moore & Kleiman Ibid.

[202] Moore and Kleiman Ibid. p 4

203 Moore and Kleiman Ibid. p 2

204 Moore and Kleiman, Ibid. p 6

205 2011 Report of Global Commission on Drug Use, Ibid. And see the Transform article on the U.K.'s evaluation of its failed law enforcement approach. Note 38 above.

206 Moore and Kleiman Ibid. p 6

207 Americans for Safe Access (2017) Memo to Congress: DEA Dumped the "Gateway-Theory" Due to Science, Retrieved from: http://www.safeaccessnow.org/memo_to_congress_dea_dumped_the_gateway_theory_due_to_science

208 Pew Research Center (2013) Majority Now Supports Legalizing Marijuana, Pew Research Center, http://www.people-press.org/2013/04/04/majority-now-supports-legalizing-marijuana/

209 Campoy, A., (2013) 'States Legalizing Recreational Marijuana Wrestle with Best Way to Test, Wall Street Journal, 8/20/2013.

210 Dalton, M. (2013) EU Seeks Action on 'Legal Highs', Wall Street Journal, U.S. Edition 9/17/2013 p A12

211 SAMHSA (2016) Ibid.

212 SAMHSA, (2016) Ibid.

213 Rosenthal, M.S. (2013) Legalizing Pot Won't Make It Any Safer. Wall Street Journal, Jan. 16,2013

214 Kevin Sabet Debates Governor Gary Johnson at Yale: https://www.youtube.com/watch?v=VABQ-XovTU0 The Legalization of Drugs (For and Against)